Mind Map AWS SAA Certification C03

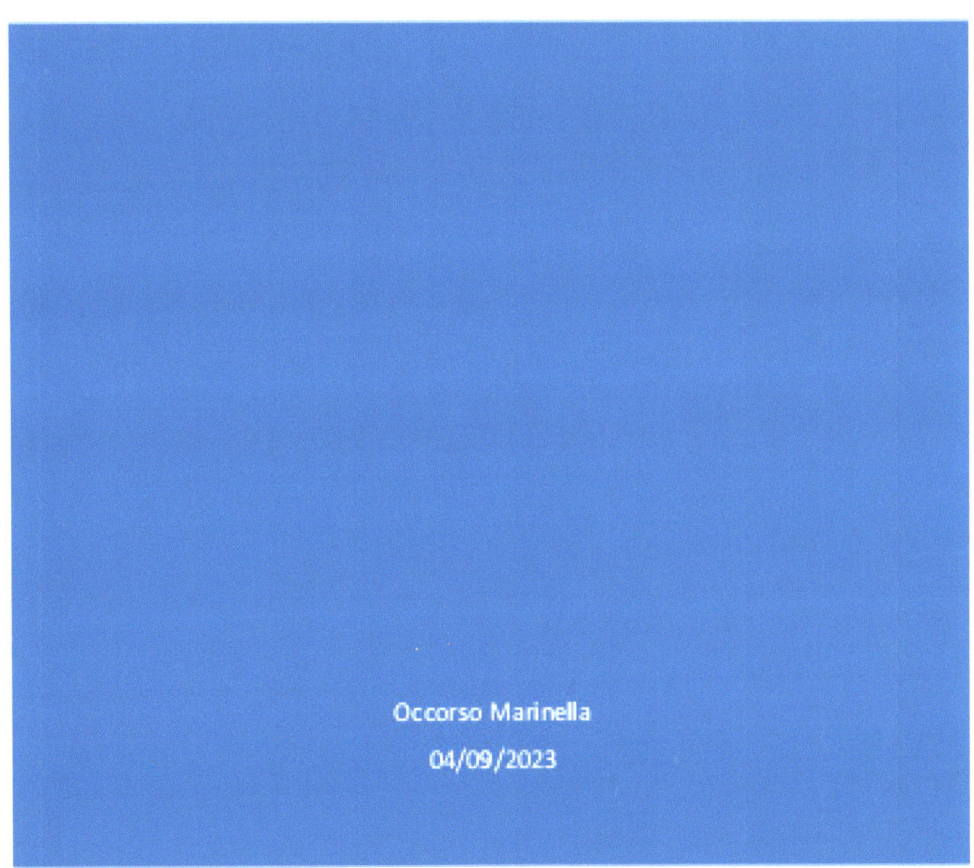

Occorso Marinella

04/09/2023

Table of Contents

2

3

Introduction

A few months ago, I recertify on AWS SAA C03 and I update this ebook to help you to memorize the concepts using mind maps.

Mind maps helped me to connect the various services together and thus have a global idea of the key topics covered.

It is assumed that before purchasing this text, a study has already been done and / or relative courses have been taken.

Basic Concepts

Global Infrastructure

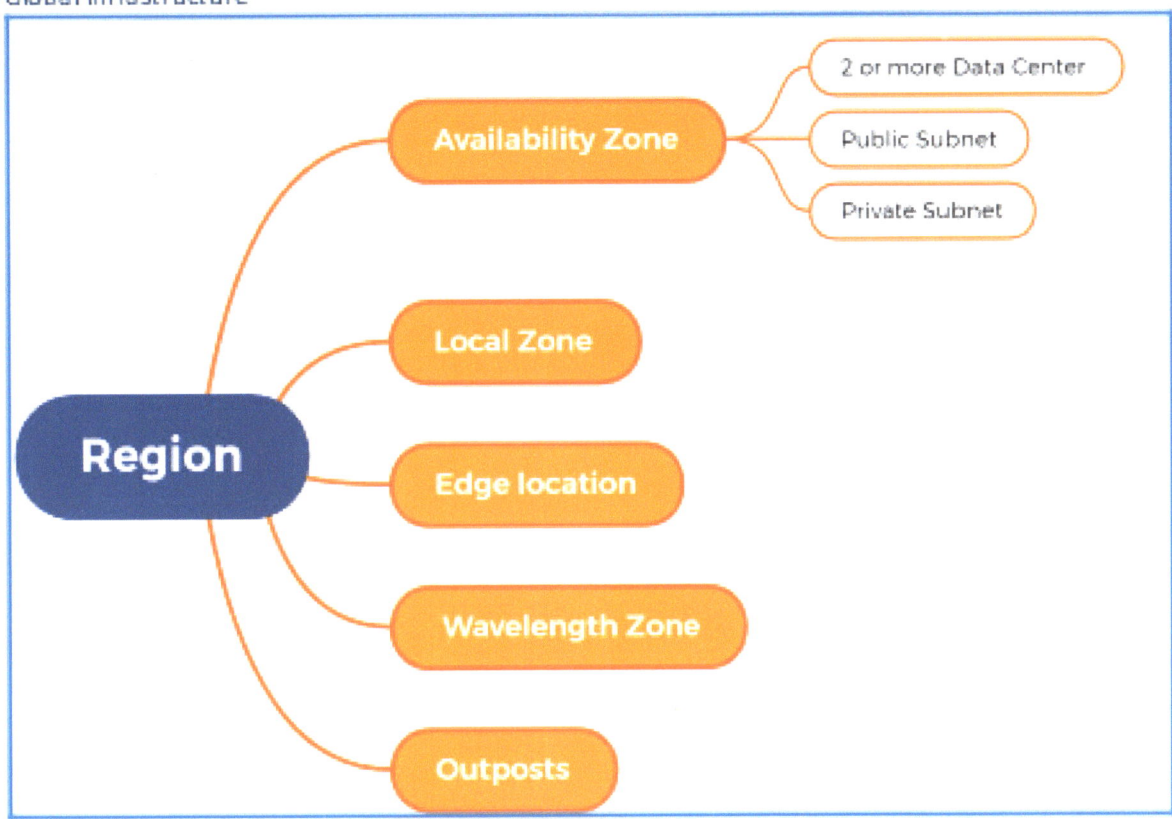

Mind Map Global Infrastructure 1

Region

- ✓ Is chosen according to the following criteria: available services, pricing proximity, laws, regulations
- ✓ Availability: global

Availability Zone

- ✓ HA inside a Region
- ✓ Availability: Up to 6 Availability Zones for each Region (a, b, c, d, e, f); minimum 3 AZ for each Region.
- ✓ The distance between two AZ must be at least 50 to 100 Km

Edge Location

- ✓ Located where there are not Region
- ✓ Used to content cache to have low latency

High Availability and Scalability

Scalability is the ability of a system to handle the increase in demand without impacting the application's performance or availability.

There are two kinds of **scalability**:

1. **Vertical**: scaling by adding more instances to your pool of resources ("scaling out")
2. **Horizontal**: scaling by adding more power (e.g. CPU, RAM) to an existing machine (also described as "scaling up")

High availability (HA) means the application remains available with no interruption after one data center (AZ) loss.

DR strategies

1. Backup & restore
2. Pilot ligt :resources activated after event
3. Warm standby: minimum of resources always running
4. Multisite active/active

DR strategies

Identity

IAM

Identity and Access Management (IAM)

It is used to securely control individual and group access to AWS resources.

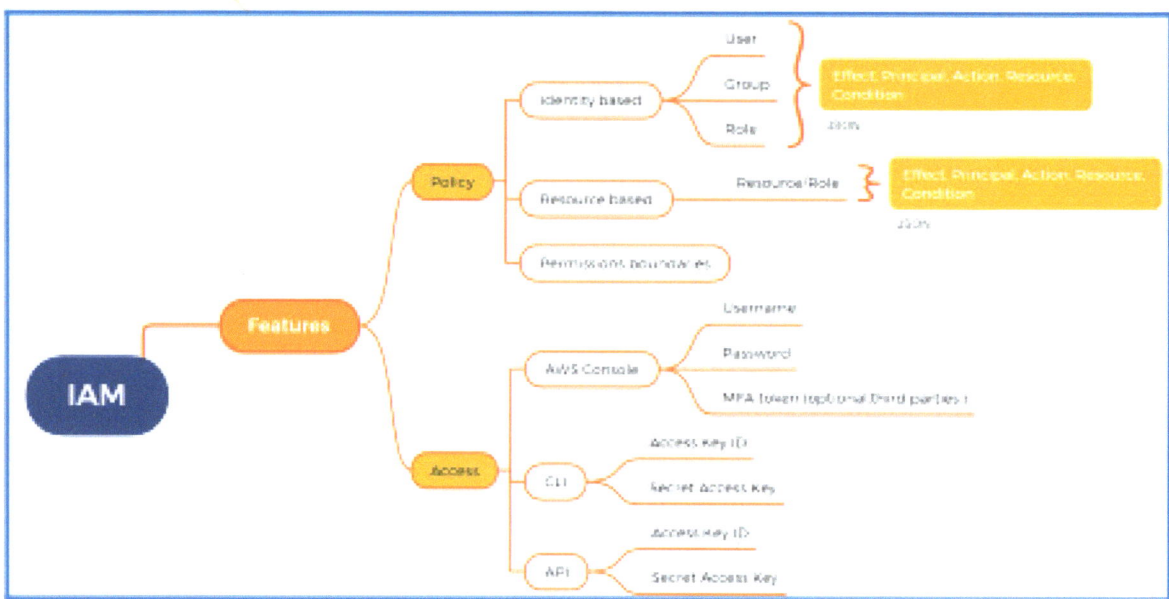

Mind Map IAM 1

Billing

Free

Operations

Managed.

Availability

Global

Remember

root account has full administrative permissions, and these cannot be restricted

9

STS

Security Token Service

Provides temporary access to AWS resources

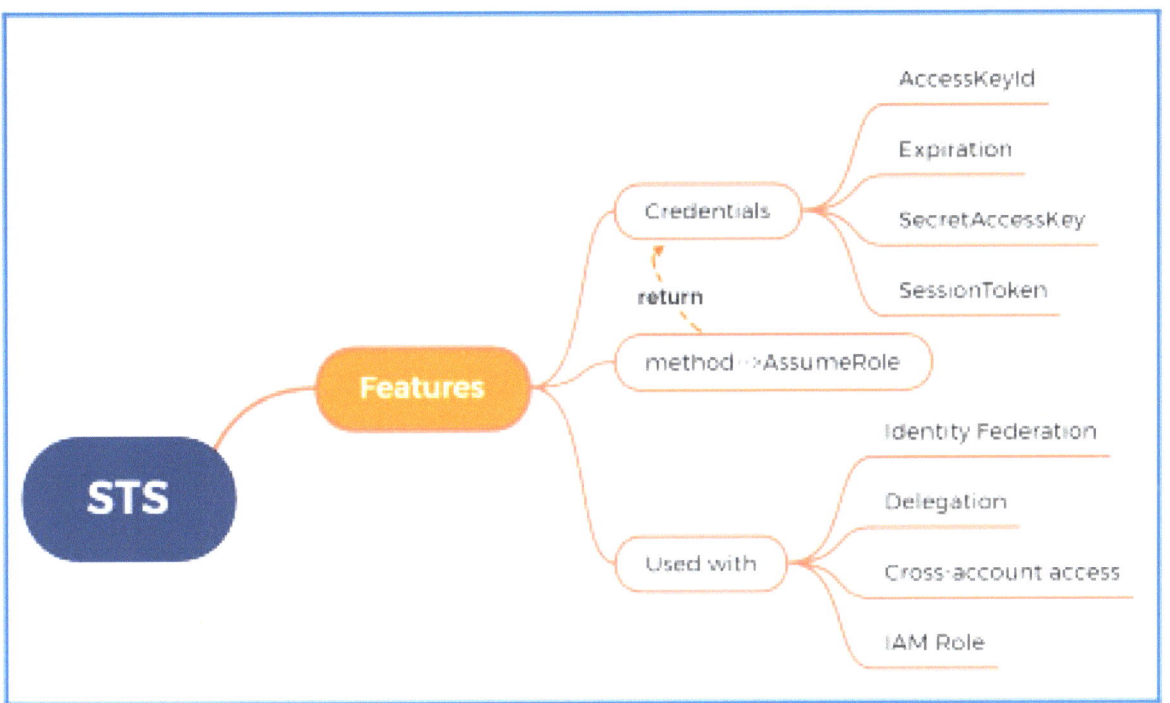

Mind Map STS 1

AWS Organization

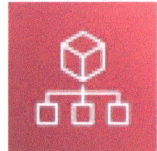

Allows to manage multiple AWS accounts, there is only one master user, the other users are members. Used to Consolidated Billing across all accounts - single payment method.

It is possible group account in Organizational Units (OUs).

Organization API used to create account programmatically and to make programmatic API call to organization.

Accounts can be migrated between organizations

Condition keys: AWS provides condition keys that you can query to provide more granular control over certain actions.

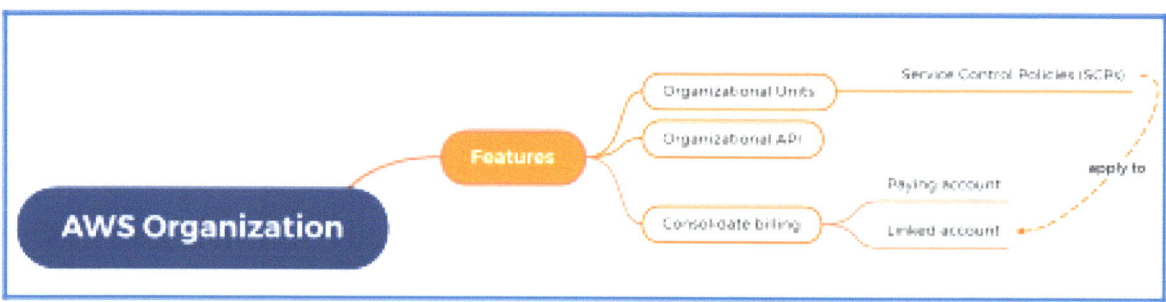

Mind Map AWS Organization 1

Availability

Global

Billing

Free

AWS Control Tower

Control Tower automates the process of setting up a new baseline multi-account AWS environment that is secure, well-architected, and ready to use.

It is an extension of OU and it sits above it.

Compute

AMI

Amazon Machine Image

Operating system installed on the VMs. By default AMI are private but can be made public. AMI can be encrypted. OS available are Linux, Microsoft Windows and MAC.

Availability

Region

EC2
Virtual Machine Instance

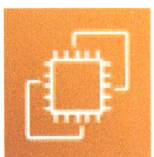

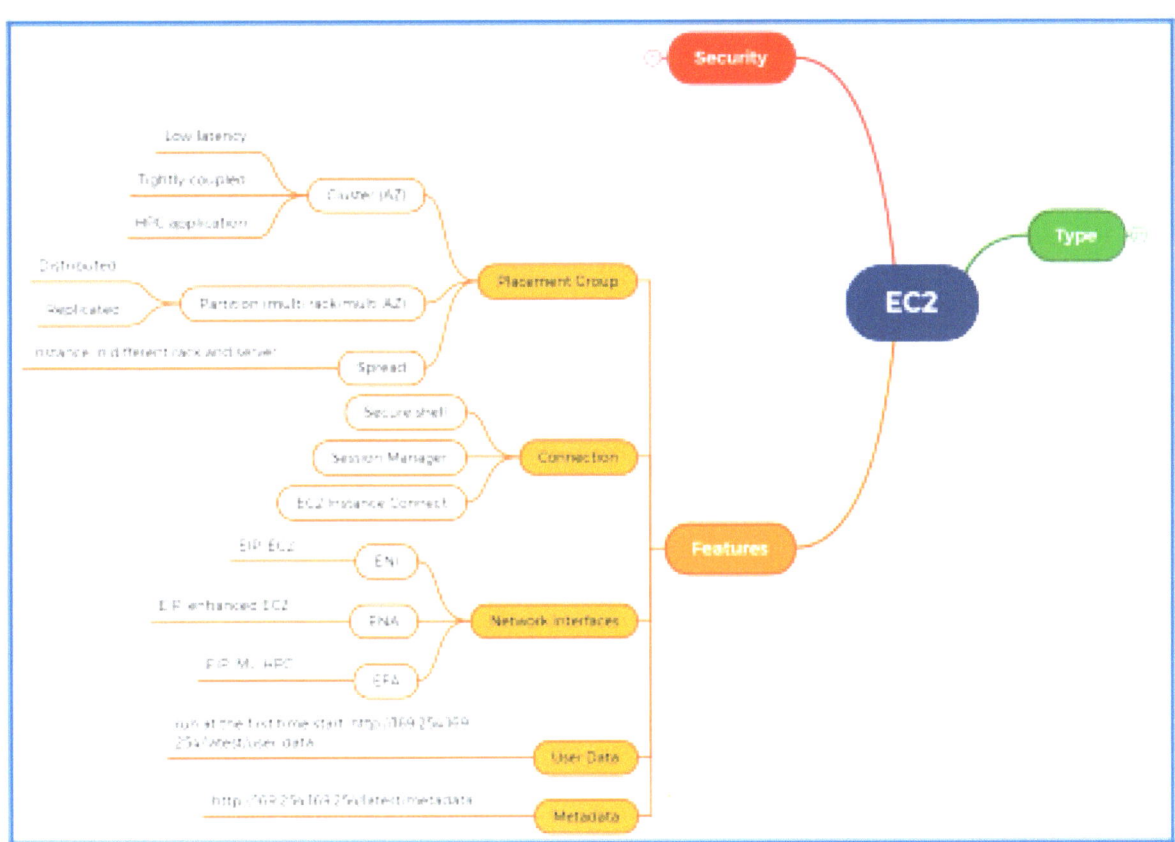

Mind Map EC2 1

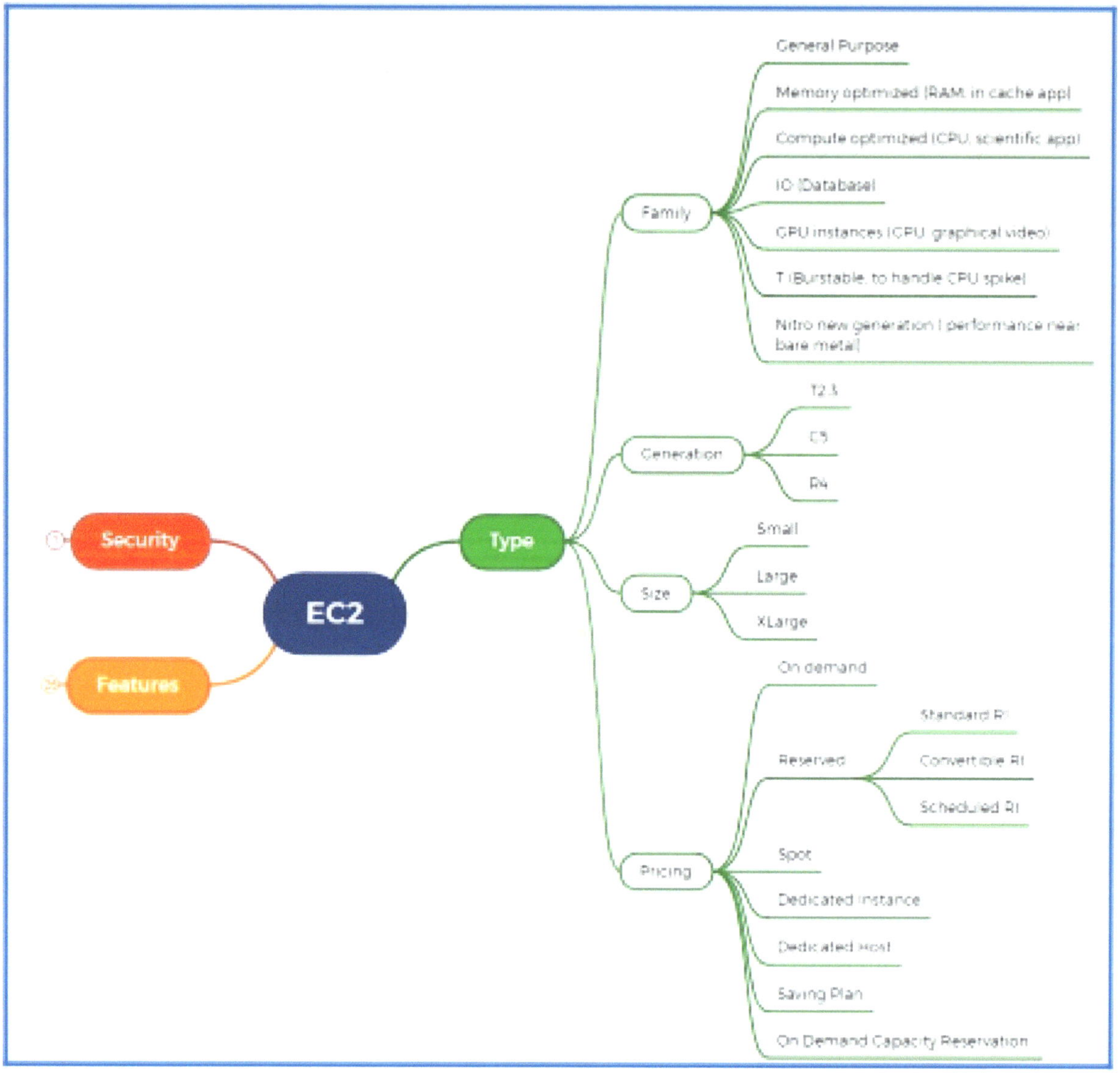

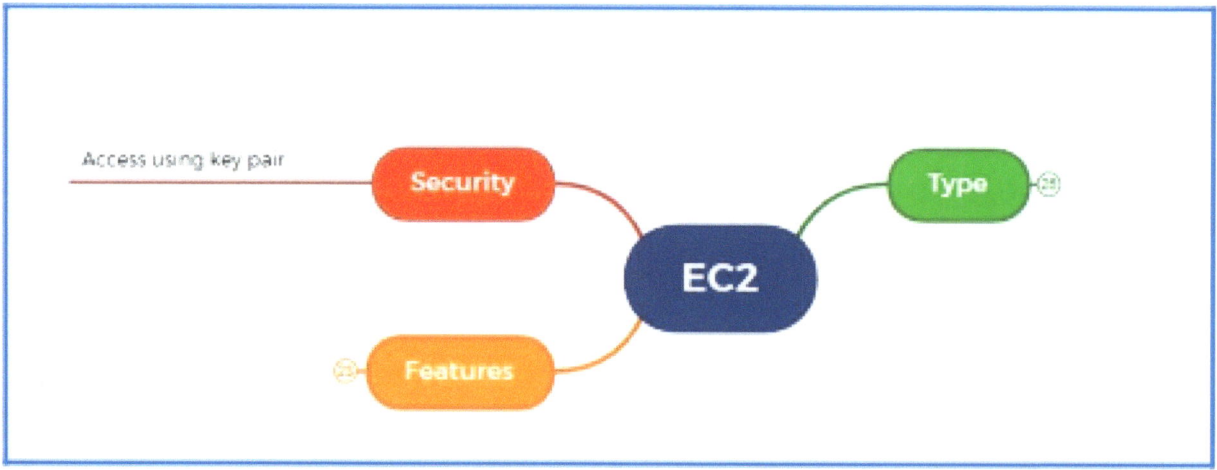

Mind Map EC2 2

```
                                                              General Purpose
                                                              Memory optimized (RAM in cache app)
                                                              Compute optimized (CPU scientific app)
                                       Family                 IO (Database)
                                                              GPU instances (GPU graphical video)
                                                              T (Burstable to handle CPU spike)
                                                              Nitro new generation (performance near
                                                              bare metal)

                                                              T2.3
                                       Generation             C5
                                                              R4
                        Type                                  Small
                                       Size                   Large
                                                              XLarge

        Security                                              On demand
                                                                            Standard RI
                                                              Reserved      Convertible RI
        EC2                                                                 Scheduled RI
                                       Pricing                Spot
                                                              Dedicated instance
        Features                                              Dedicated Host
                                                              Saving Plan
                                                              On Demand Capacity Reservation
```

Mind Map EC2 2

```
    Access using key pair        Security                        Type

                                            EC2

                                 Features
```

Mind Map EC2 3

Availability

AZ

<u>Billing</u>

Per second for on demand and spot instances

<u>Details:</u>

Tag: it is possible tag an EC2 Instance. Tag is a metadata.

IP: By default, EC2 instances have N°1 Public IP (IP change if we restart the instance) and N°1 Private IP. We can also assign an **Elastic IP** (this IP does not change if we restart the Instance, it is a fix IP and we can move it between different EC2 instances and different AZ). Max N°5 Elastic IP for each account. Charged if not used.

ENI: Basic virtual network card. It can have:

- One Primary private IPv4, one or more secondary IPv4
- One Elastic IP (IPv4) per private IPv4
- One Public IPv4
- One or more security groups
- One MAC address
- Scope: AZ
- It is possible move an ENI between two EC2
- Supported by all EC2 instance type

ENA: Enhanced networking performance

- Supported by a set of instances type EC2

EFA: Enhanced networking performance

- Supported by all instances type EC2
- Used with HPC and ML

Security group: they control the traffic in and out of EC2 in terms of ports and protocol enabled, from a source to a destination. A security group can point to a subnet or a security group.

EC2 Hibernate: The in-memory (RAM) state is preserved so the instances boot is faster. the RAM state is written to a file in the EBS volume.

16

Lambda

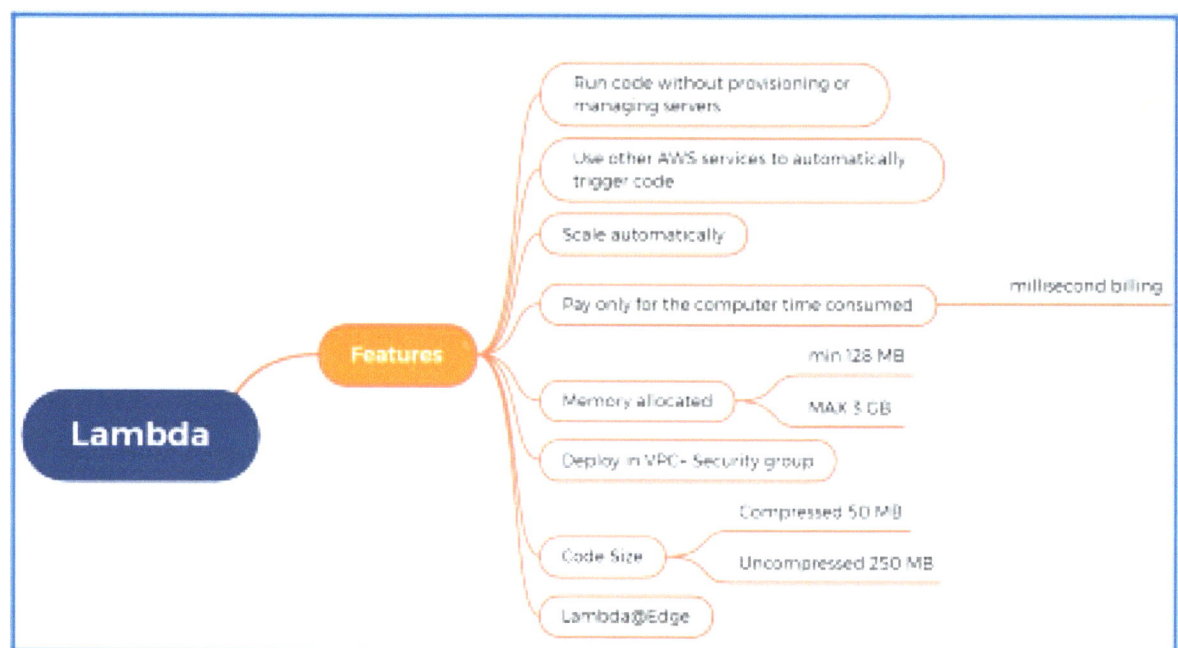

To run code without provisioning or managing servers

Mind Map Lambda 1

Billing

Pay per call and pay per duration.

Operations

Managed.

Storage

EBS

EC2 Storage, block storage.

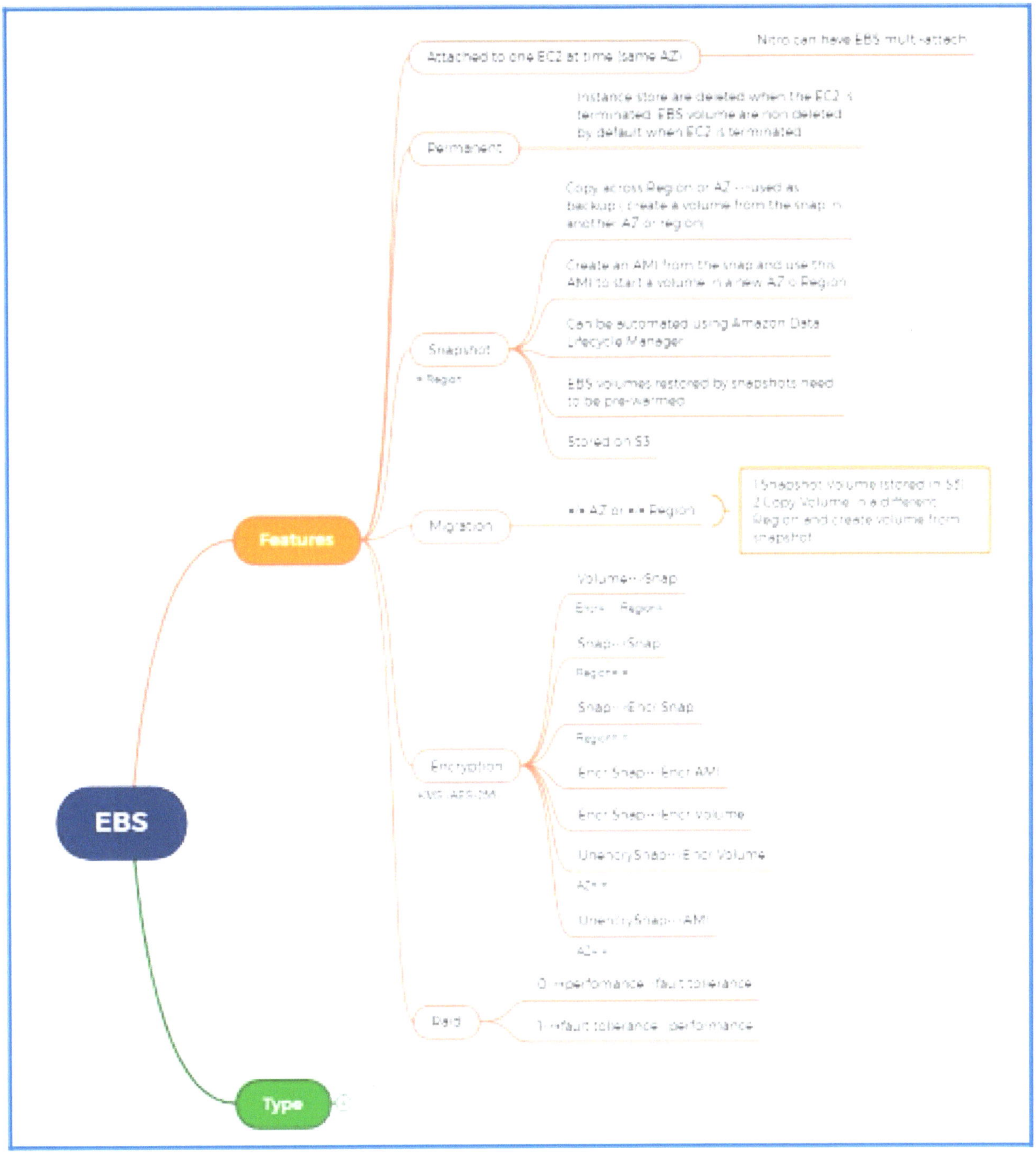

Features
- Attached to one EC2 at time (same AZ) — Nitro can have EBS multi-attach
- Permanent — Instance store are deleted when the EC2 is terminated. EBS volume are non deleted by default when EC2 is terminated
- Snapshot
  - Region
    - Copy across Region or AZ — used as backup (create a volume from the snap in another AZ or region)
    - Create an AMI from the snap and use this AMI to start a volume in a new AZ o Region
    - Can be automated using Amazon Data Lifecycle Manager
    - EBS volumes restored by snapshots need to be pre-warmed
    - Stored on S3
- Migration — ** AZ or ** Region
  - 1 Snapshot volume (stored in S3)
  - 2 Copy Volume in a different Region and create volume from snapshot
- Encryption
  - KMS AES-256
    - Volume → Snap
    - Encr → Region —
    - Snap → Snap
    - Region **
    - Snap → Encr Snap
    - Region **
    - Encr Snap → Encr AMI
    - Encr Snap → Encr Volume
    - Unencry Snap → Encr Volume
    - AZ **
    - Unencry Snap → AMI
    - AZ **
- Raid
  - 0 - performance - fault tolerance
  - 1 - fault tolerance - performance

EBS

Type

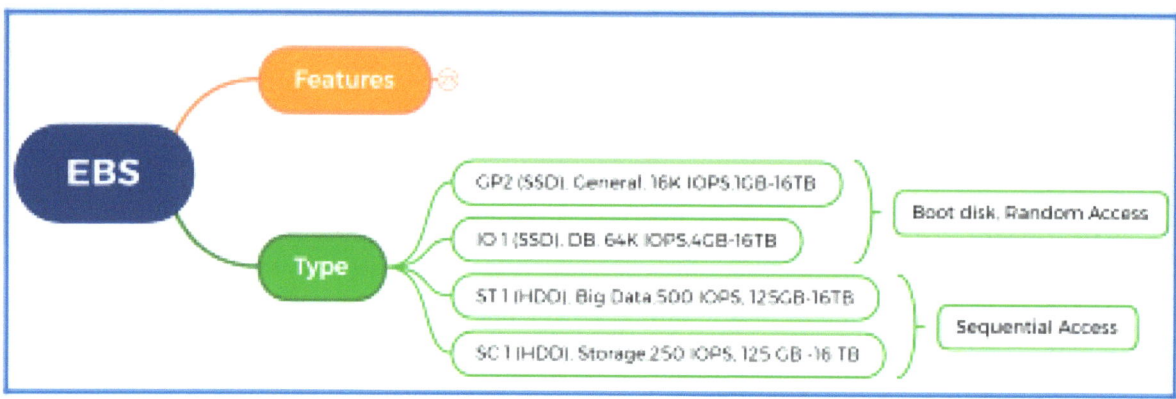

Mind Map EBS 2

Billing

Based on EBS type.

Operations

Unmanaged.

Availability

AZ

EFS

EC2 Storage, NFS for Linux, mounted on many EC2 at time

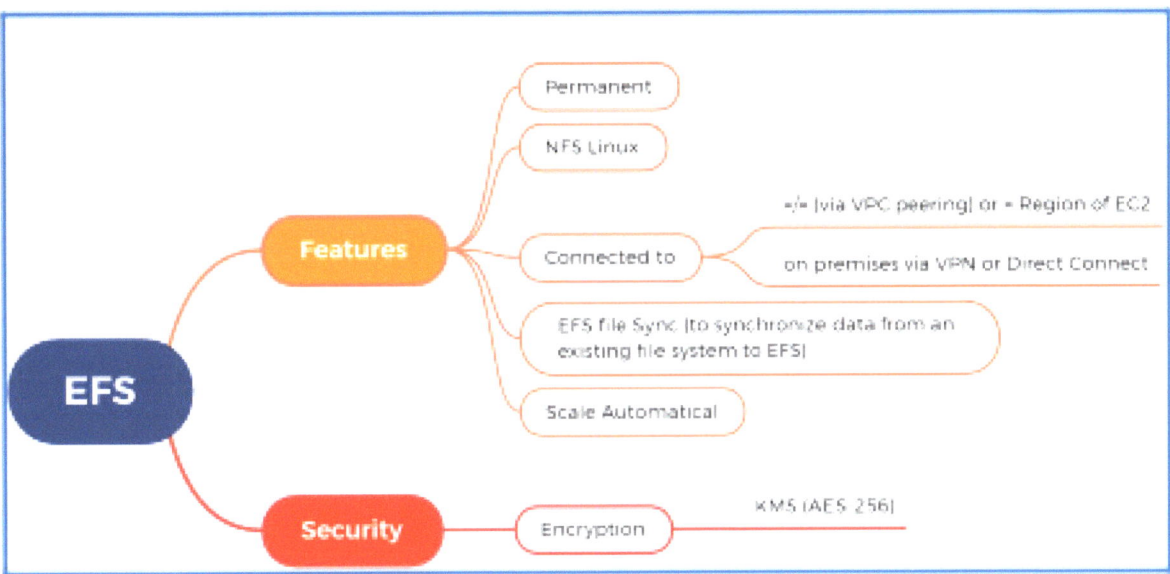

Mind Map EFS 1

Billing

More expensive than EBS

Operations

Managed.

Availability

MultiAZ

FSX

File Server for Windows (SMB)

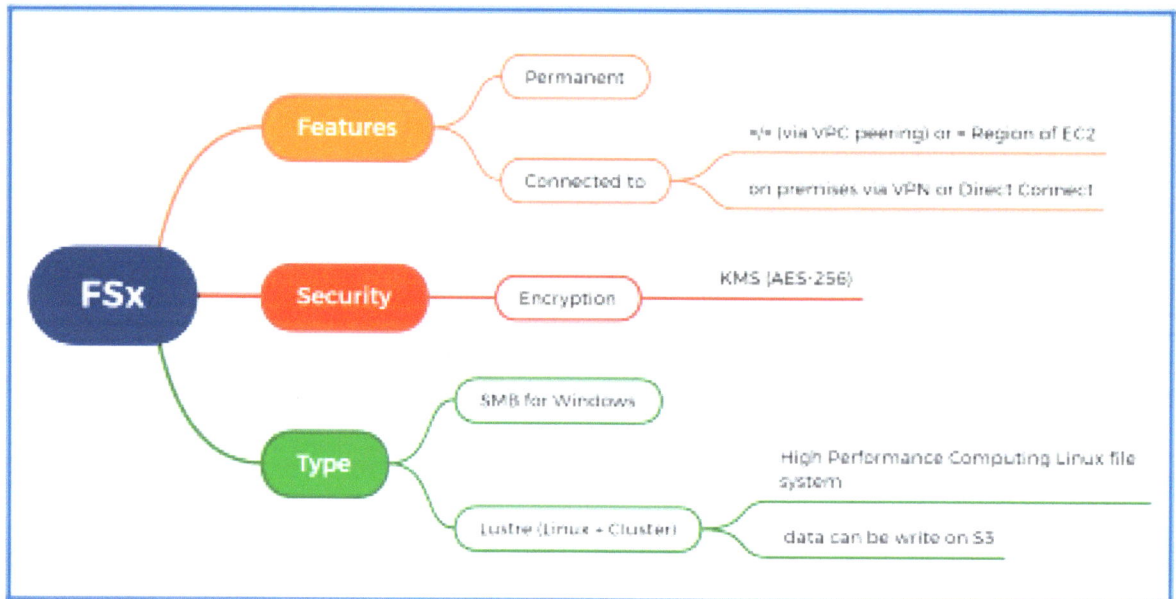

Mind Map FSx 1

<u>Billing</u>

More expensive than EBS

<u>Operations</u>

Managed.

<u>Availability</u>

MutiAZ or AZ

S3

Object Storage

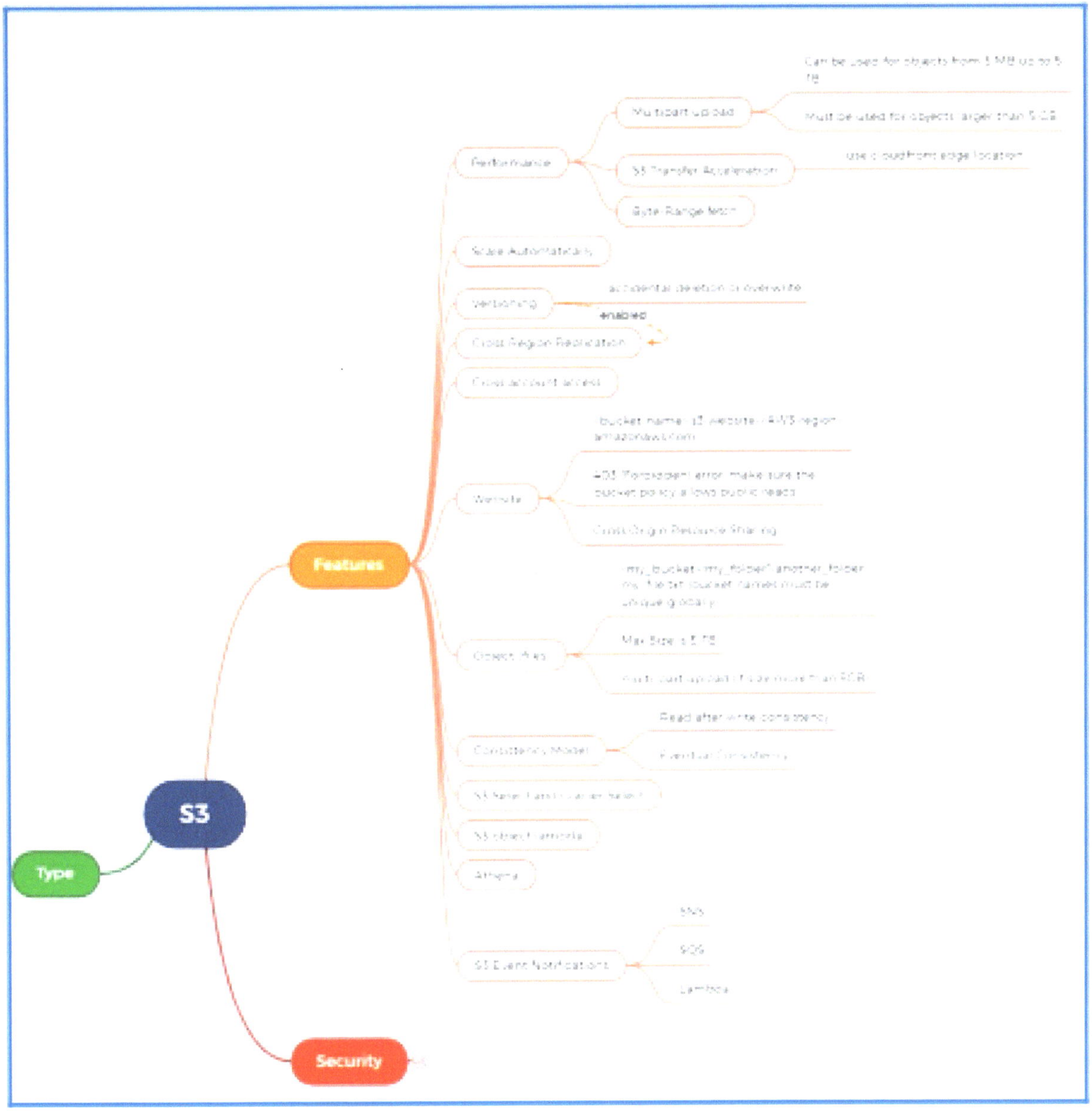

Mind Map S3 1

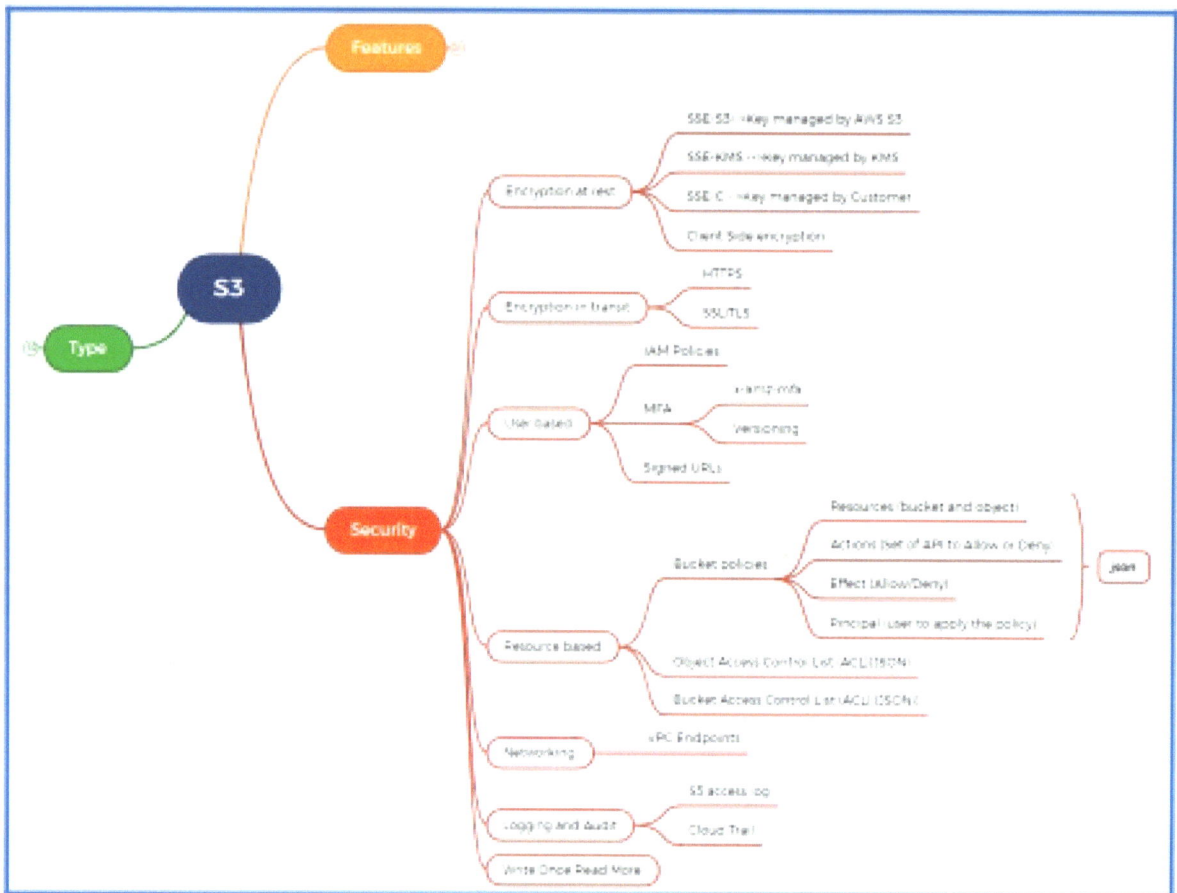

Mind Map S3 2

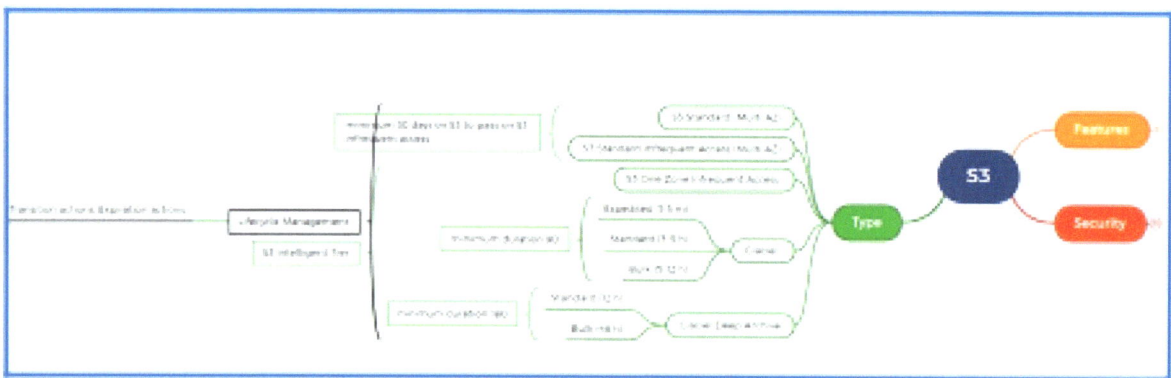

Mind Map S3 3

Billing

Based on object size, S3 type, storage duration.

Operations

Unmanaged.

Availability

Region but Buckets must have a globally unique name

Snow Family

Migrate data from on prem to AWS

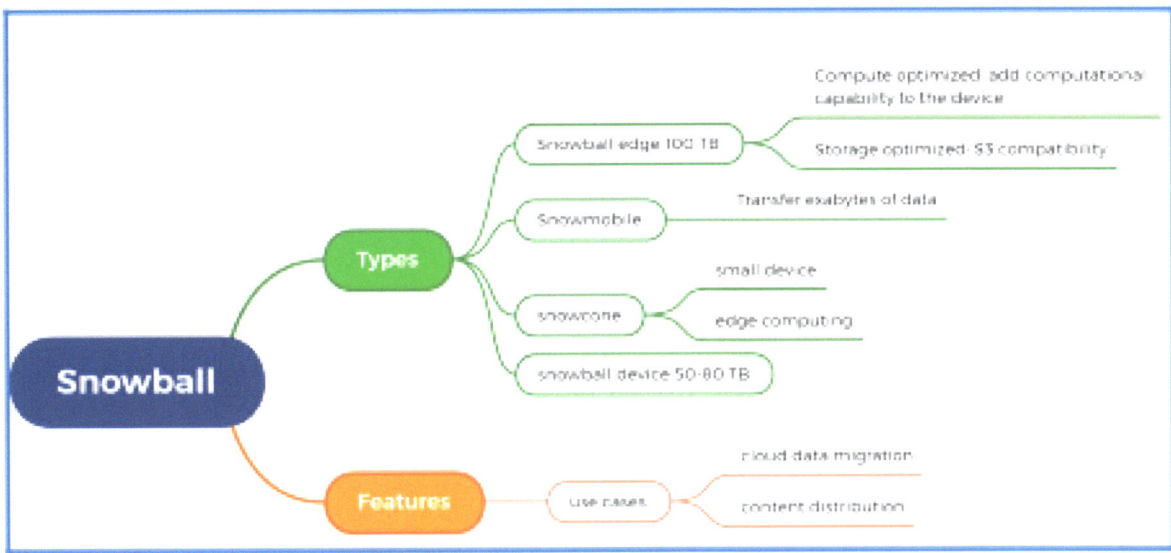

Mind Map AWS Snow Family 1

Snowball

The AWS Snowball service uses physical storage devices to transfer large amounts of data between Amazon Simple Storage Service (Amazon S3) and your onsite data storage location at faster-than-internet speeds.

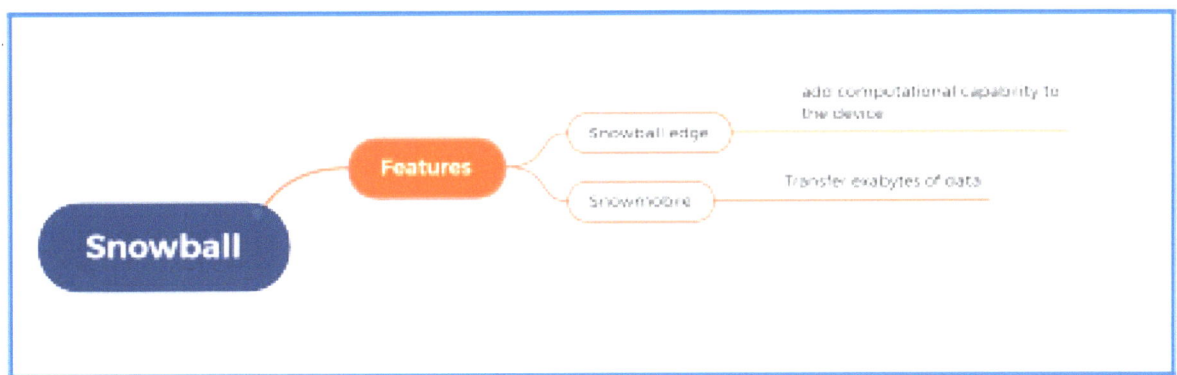

Mind Map Snowball 1

Storge Gateway

Bridge between on-premise Storage and cloud data in S3

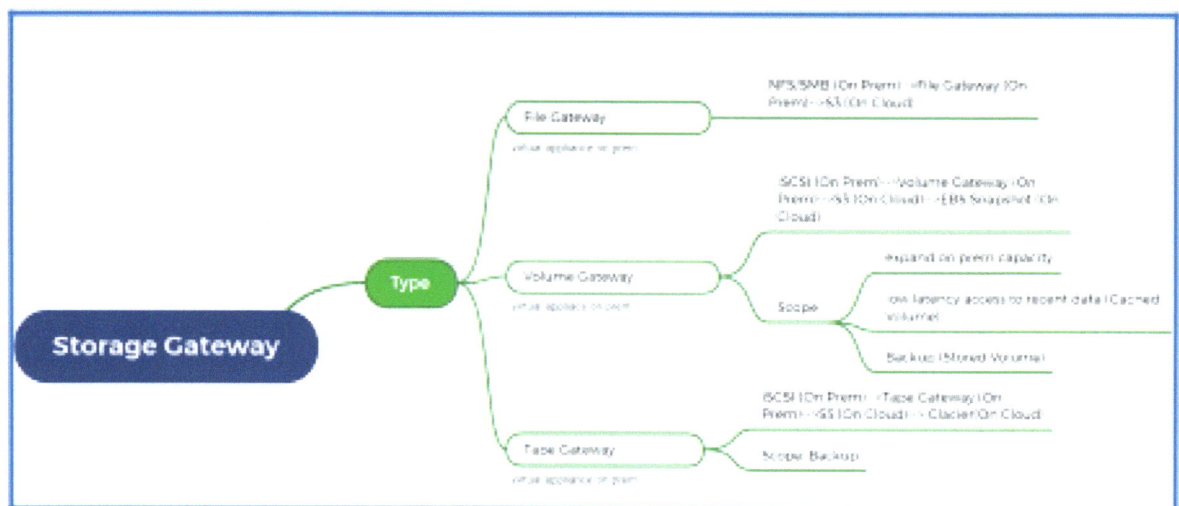

Mind Map Storage Gateway 1

Container

ECS

Amazon Elastic Container Service (Amazon ECS) is a highly scalable, fast, container management service.
Helps to run Docker containers on EC2

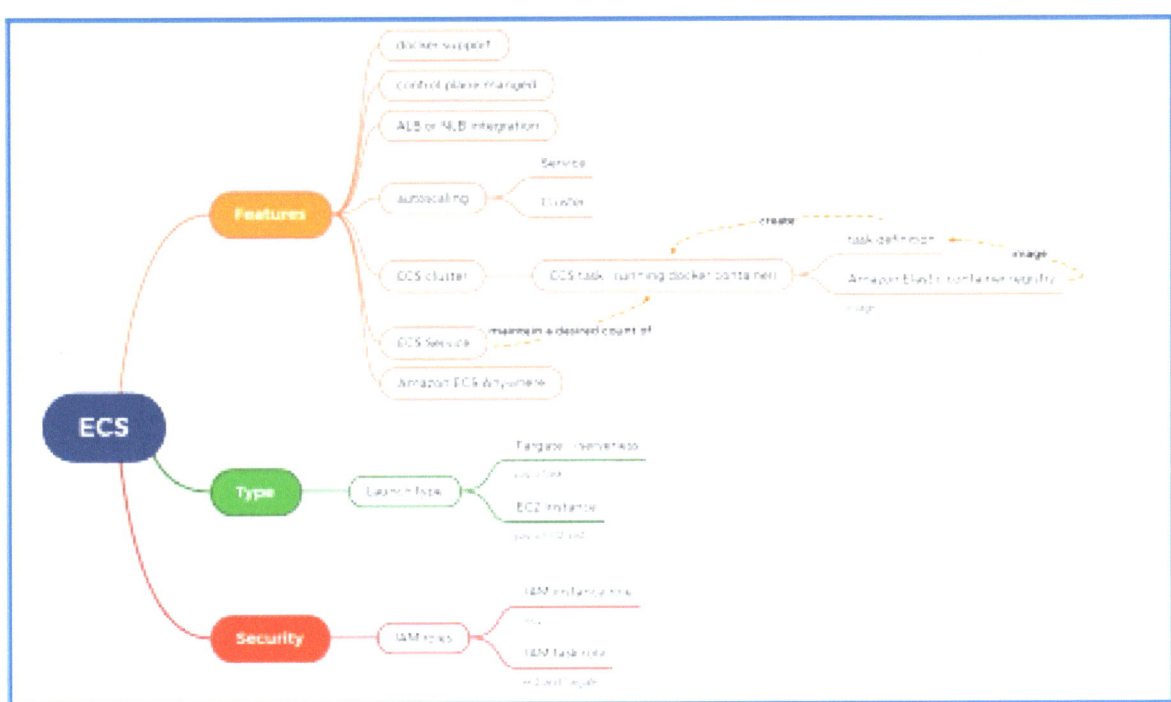

Mind Map ECS 1

Availability

Multi AZ

EKS

Amazon Elastic Kubernetes Service (Amazon EKS) is a managed service that makes it easy for you to run Kubernetes on AWS

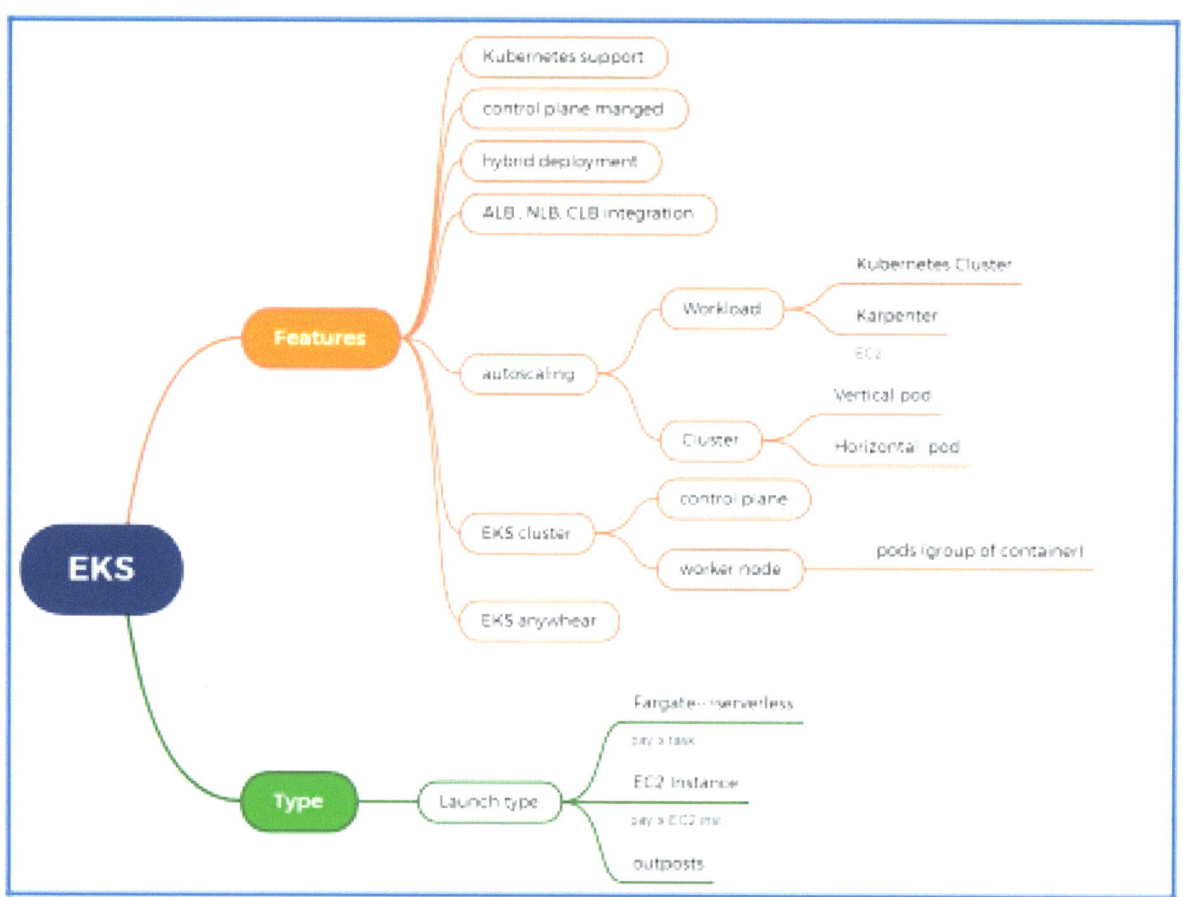

Mind Map EKS 1

ECR

Amazon ECR is a fully managed container registry offering high-performance hosting, so you can reliably deploy application images and artifacts anywhere. Integrated with ECS e EKS.

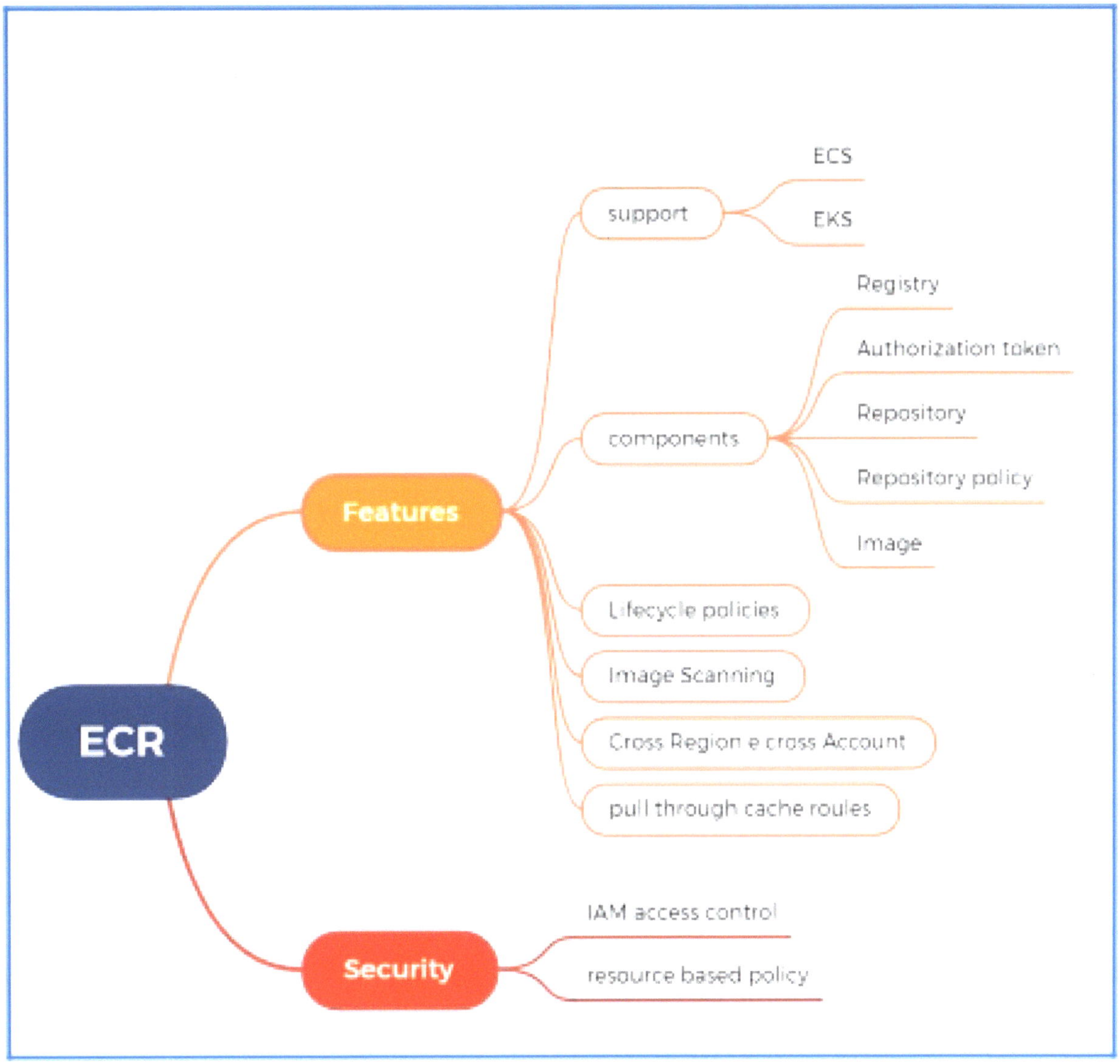

- ECR
  - Features
    - support
      - ECS
      - EKS
    - components
      - Registry
      - Authorization token
      - Repository
      - Repository policy
      - Image
    - Lifecycle policies
    - Image Scanning
    - Cross Region e cross Account
    - pull through cache roules
  - Security
    - IAM access control
    - resource based policy

Mind Map ECR 1

28

AWS APP RUNNER

AWS App Runner is a fully managed container application service that lets you build, deploy, and run containerized web applications and API services.

PAAS Solution

Database and Data Warehouse

RDS

Relational Database Service

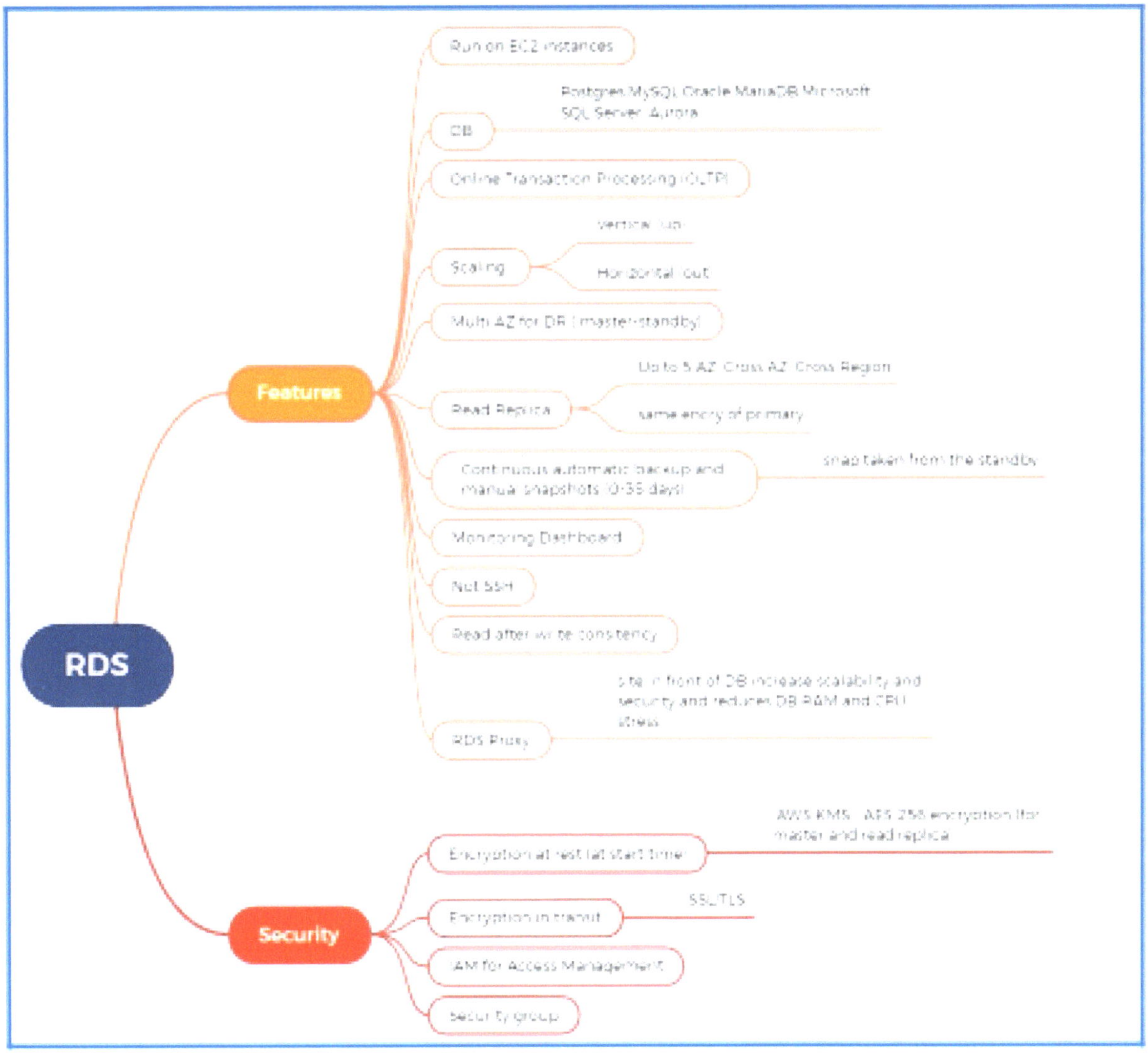

Run on EC2 instances

Postgres MySQL Oracle MariaDB Microsoft SQL Server Aurora

DB

Online Transaction Processing (OLTP)

Vertical (up)

Scaling

Horizontal (out)

Multi AZ for DR (master-standby)

Up to 5 AZ Cross AZ Cross Region

Features

Read Replica

same memory of primary

Continuous automatic backup and manual snapshots (0-35 days)

snap taken from the standby

Monitoring Dashboard

Not SSH

Read after write consistency

site in front of DB increase scalability and security and reduces DB RAM and CPU stress

RDS Proxy

RDS

AWS KMS - AES 256 encryption (for master and read replica

Encryption at rest (at start time)

Security

Encryption in transit

SSL TLS

IAM for Access Management

security group

Mind Map RDS 1

Billing

Read replica cross AZ more expensive than same AZ

Operations

Managed.

<u>Remember</u>

- You can only enable encryption for an Amazon RDS DB instance when you create it, not after the DB instance is created
- DB instances that are encrypted can't be modified to disable encryption
- You can't have:
    - An encrypted read replica of an unencrypted DB instance
    - An unencrypted read replica of an encrypted DB instance
- You can't restore an unencrypted backup or snapshot to an encrypted DB instance

AURORA

Relational Database Service, proprietary technology from AWS

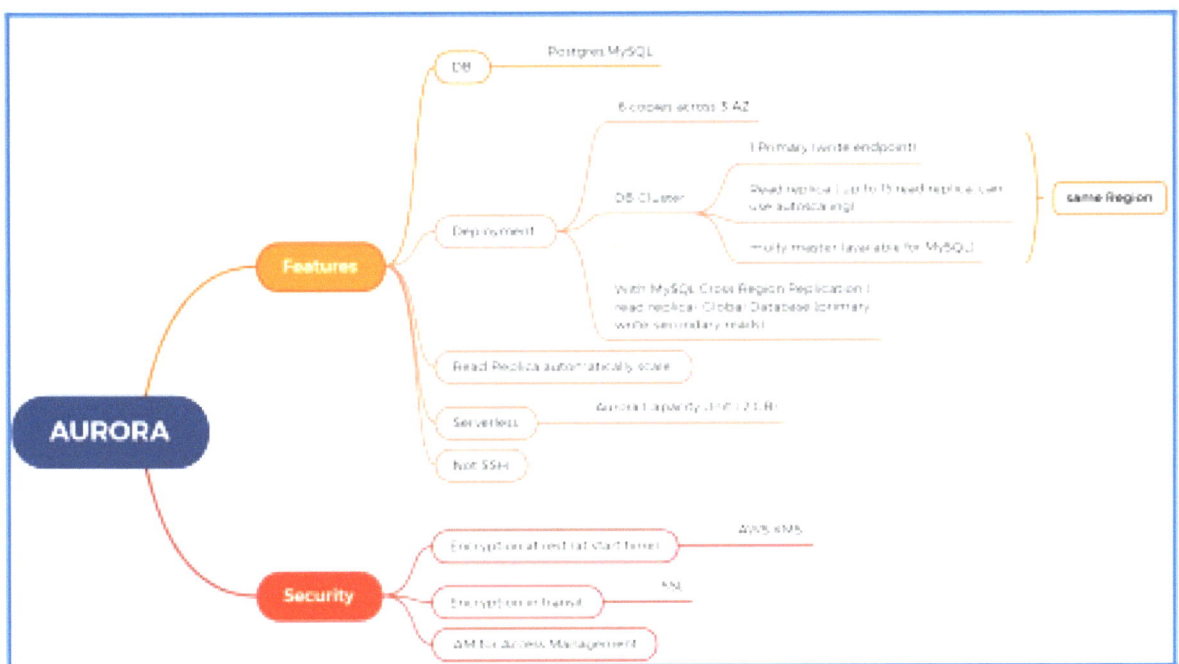

Mind Map AURORA 1

Availability

Global

Billing

pay per second, more expensive

DynamoDB

Amazon DynamoDB is a fully managed NoSQL database

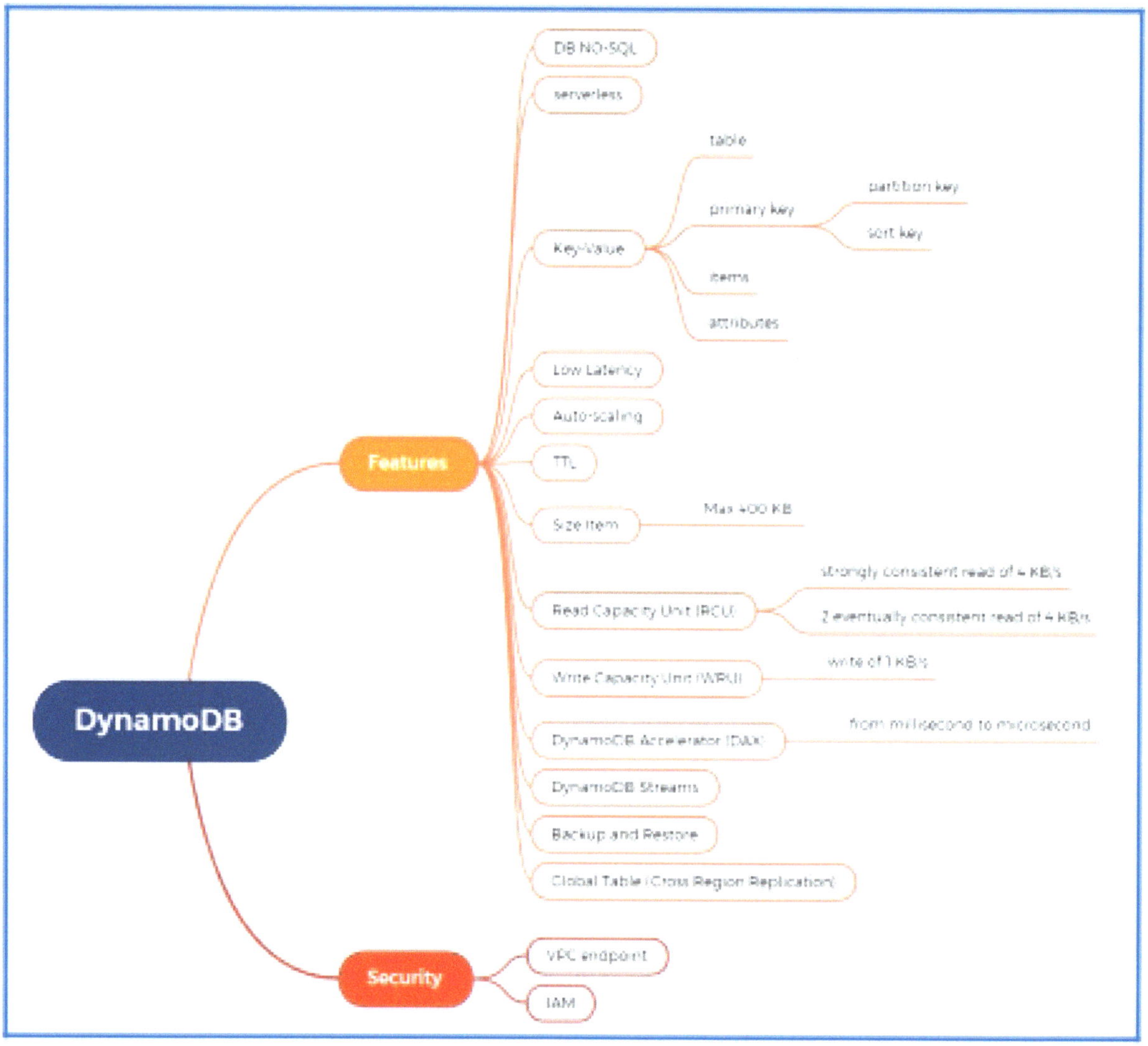

```
                                          DB NO-SQL
                                          serverless
                                                            table
                                                            primary key          partition key
                                          Key-Value                               sort key
                                                            items
                                                            attributes
                                          Low Latency
                                          Auto-scaling
                         Features         TTL
                                                            Max 400 KB
                                          Size Item
                                                            strongly consistent read of 4 KB/s
                                          Read Capacity Unit (RCU)
                                                            2 eventually consistent read of 4 KB/s
   DynamoDB                               Write Capacity Unit (WRU)    write of 1 KB/s
                                          DynamoDB Accelerator (DAX)    from millisecond to microsecond
                                          DynamoDB Streams
                                          Backup and Restore
                                          Global Table (Cross Region Replication)
                                                            VPC endpoint
                         Security
                                                            IAM
```

Mind Map DynamoDB 1

Availability

Replicate in 3 AZ /Global (Multi Region)

Operation:

Managed

Elasticache

In memory DB

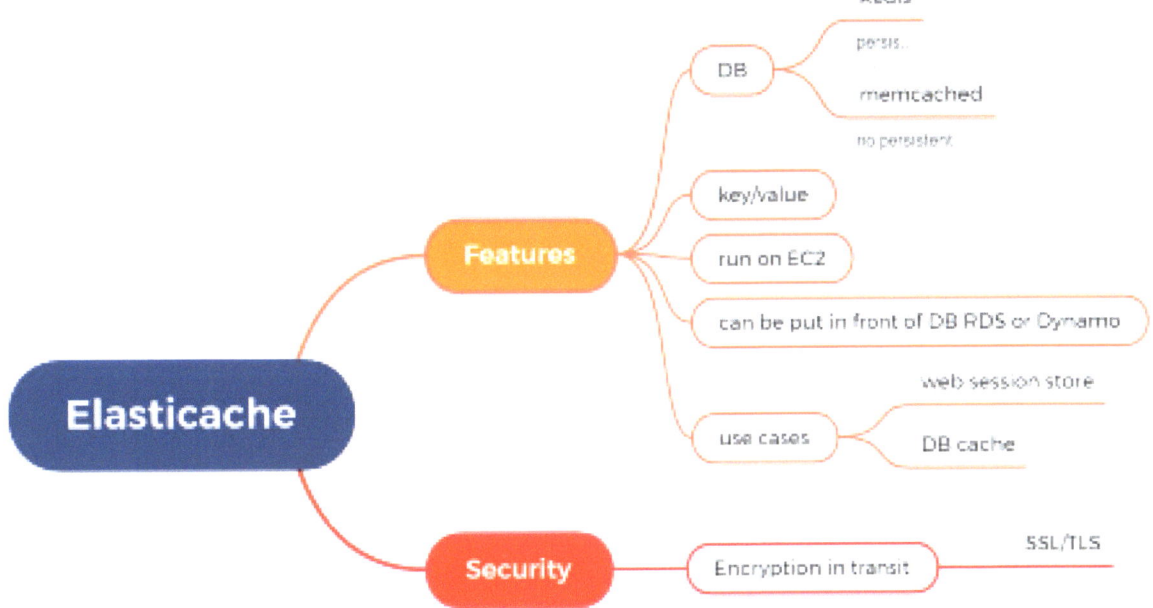

Mind Map Elasticache 1

Availability

MultiAZ

Redshift

Analytics / BI / SQL based Data Warehouse

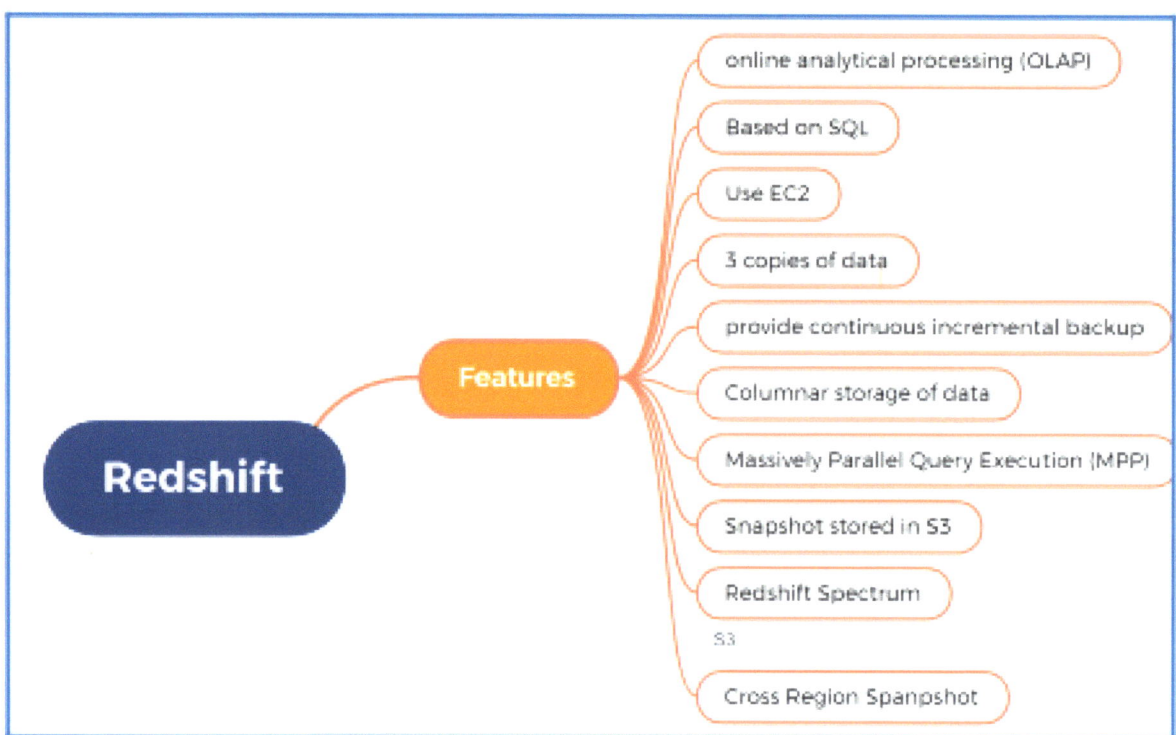

Mind Map Redshift 1

Amazon EMR

Amazon EMR is a cloud **big data** platform (including Apache Hadoop and Spark) for running large-scale distributed data processing jobs, interactive SQL queries, and machine learning applications

Kinesis

Amazon Kinesis Data Streams collect and process large streams of data records in real time.

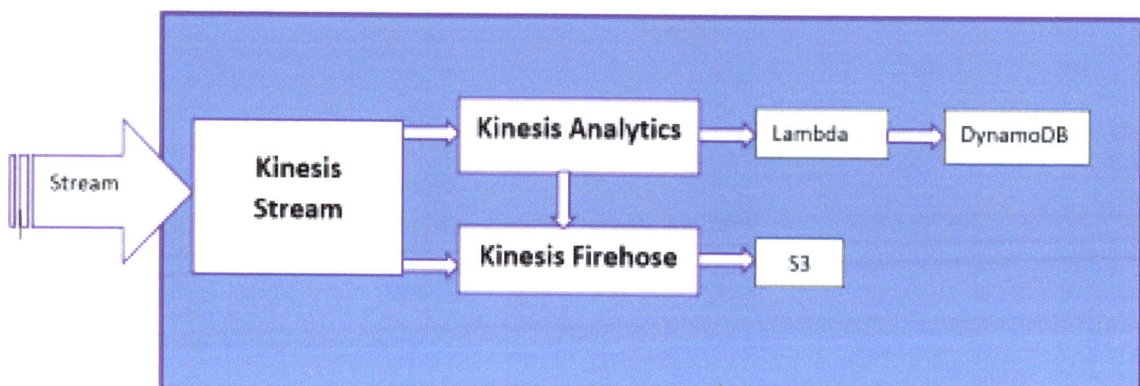

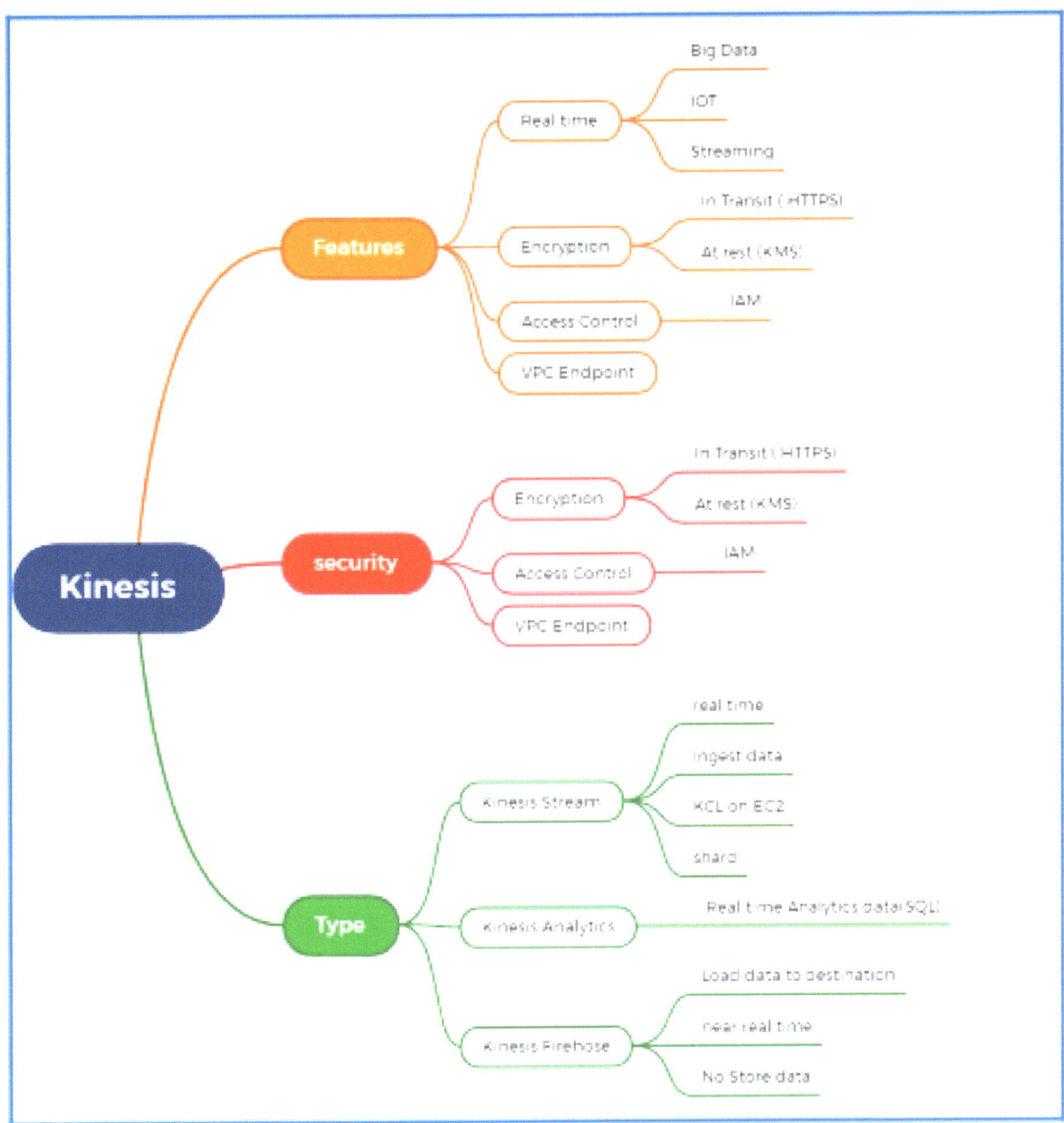

Mind Map Kinesis 1

Availability

 Automatically replicate in 3 AZ

Type

 Pull, more consumer, data do not delete after consumed

Athena

Fully Serverless database with SQL capabilities. Athena provides a simplified, flexible way to analyze petabytes of data where it lives. Analyze data or build applications from an Amazon S3

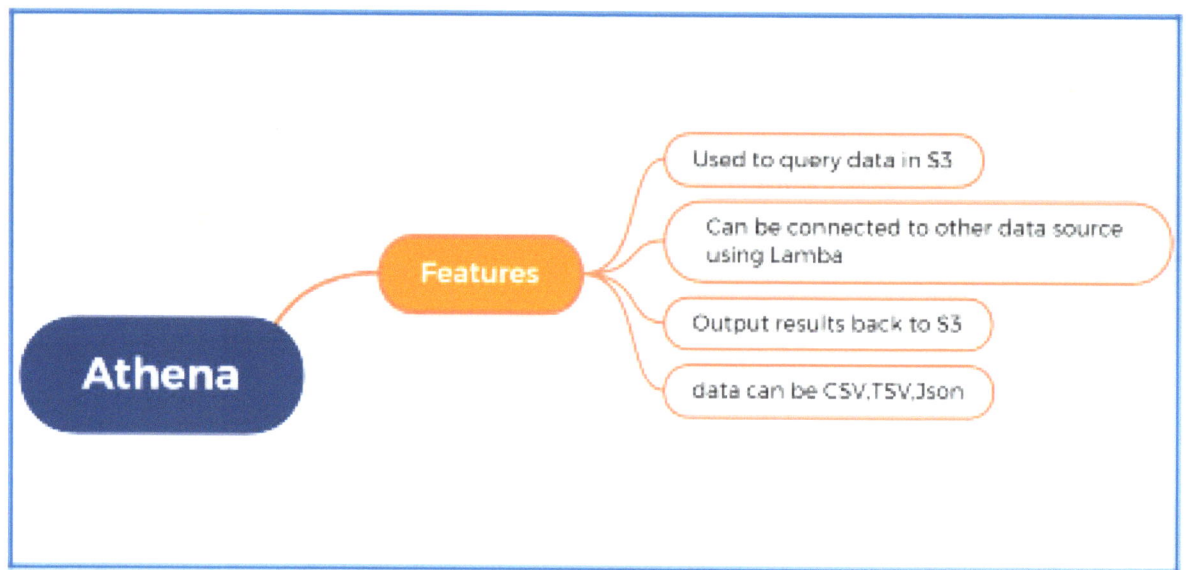

Mind Map Athena 1

Billing
Pay per query

GLUE

Serverless, used as metadata catalog. ETL (Extract, Transform, Load). AWS Glue tracks data that has already been processed during previous run of ETL job by persisting state information from the job run. This is called "job bookmarks."

Opensearch

It is a fully managed service that enables you to search, visualize and analyze text and unstructured data.

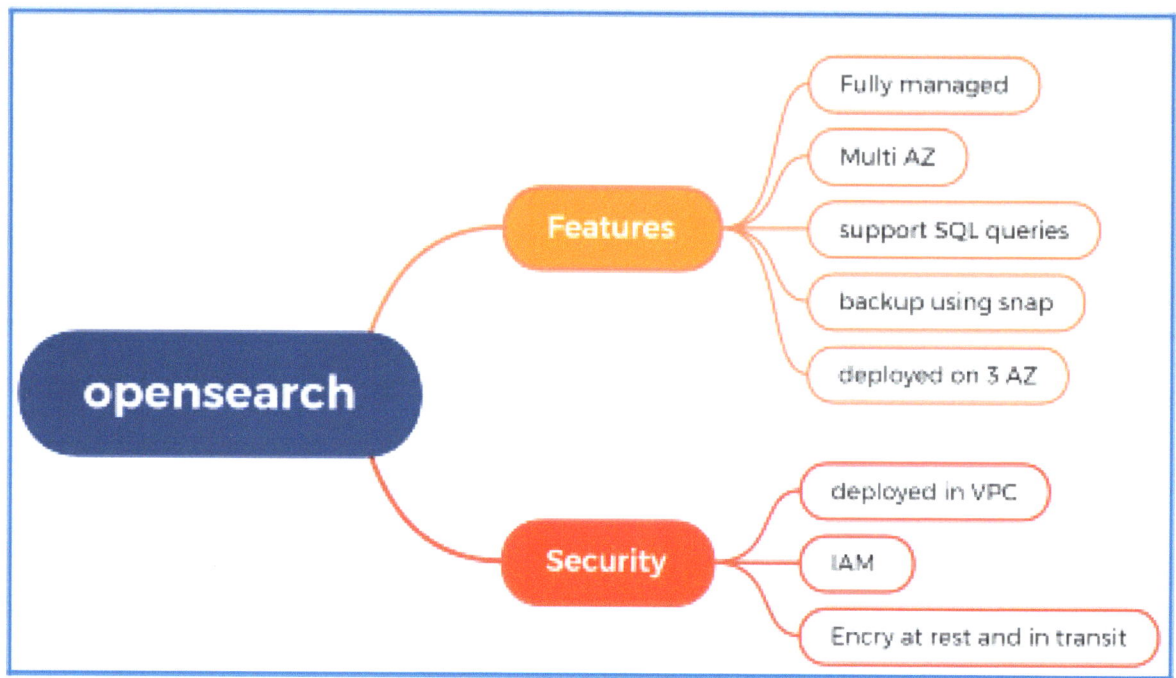

Mind Map opensearch 1

Document DB

It provides MongoDB compatible DB

Keyspaces

It provides Apache Cassandra compatible DB

Neptune

Amazon Neptune is a fast, reliable, fully managed graph database service (Social Network, Wikipedia)

Timestream

DB service for IOT

Data Lake

It is a centralized repository that allow you to store all your structured and unstructured data. Can create dashboard.

Lake formation

Enable to setup secure data lake

QuickSight

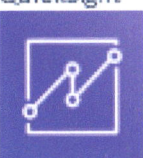

It is used to create interactive dashboards from S3, RDS, Redshift, Aurora, Athena and Opensearch.

Network

VPC

Amazon Virtual Private Cloud (Amazon VPC) enables you to provision a logically isolated section of the AWS Cloud where you can launch AWS resources in a virtual network that you've defined.

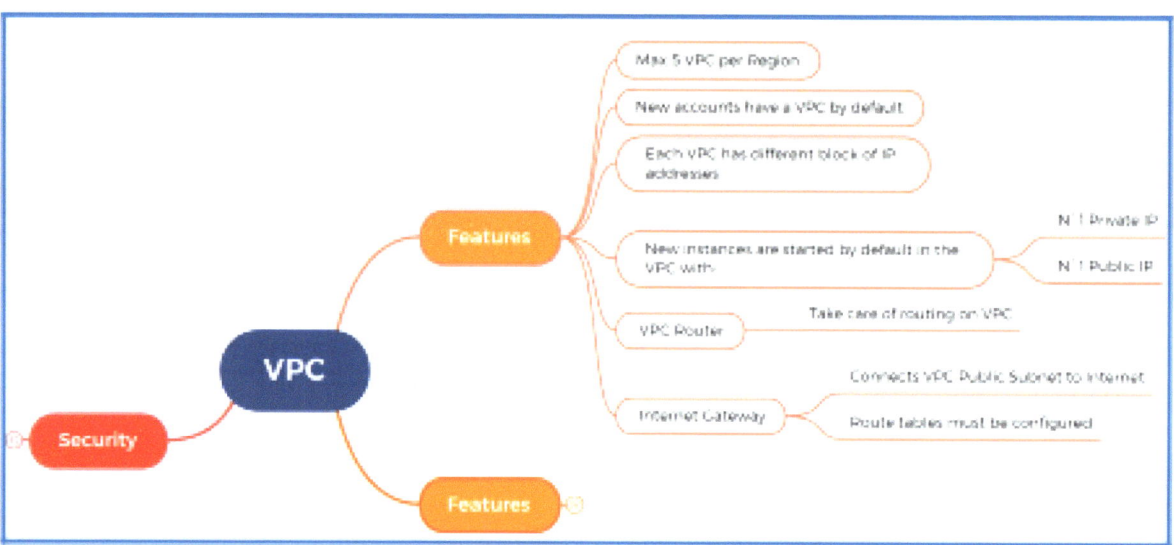

VPC 1

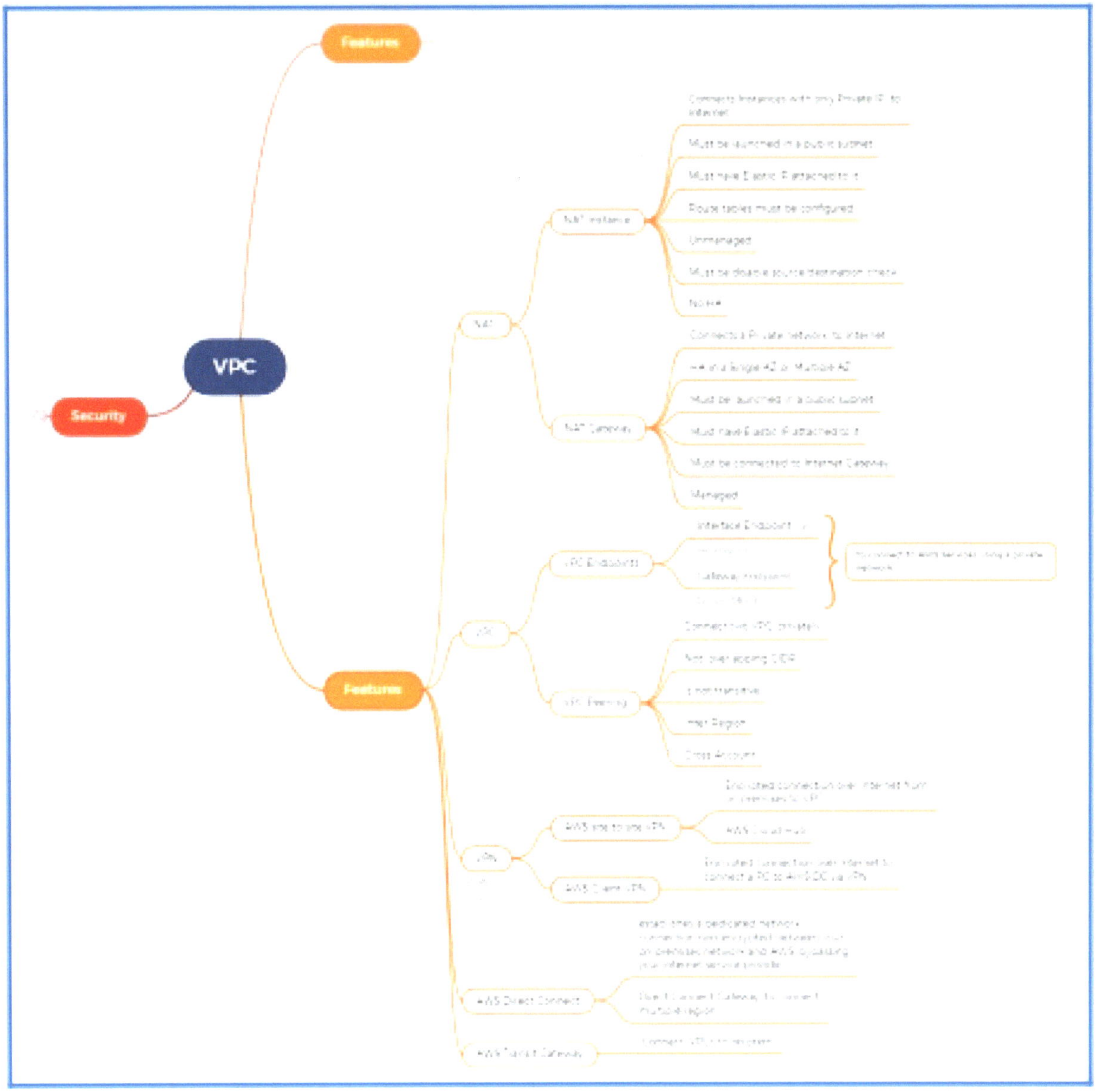

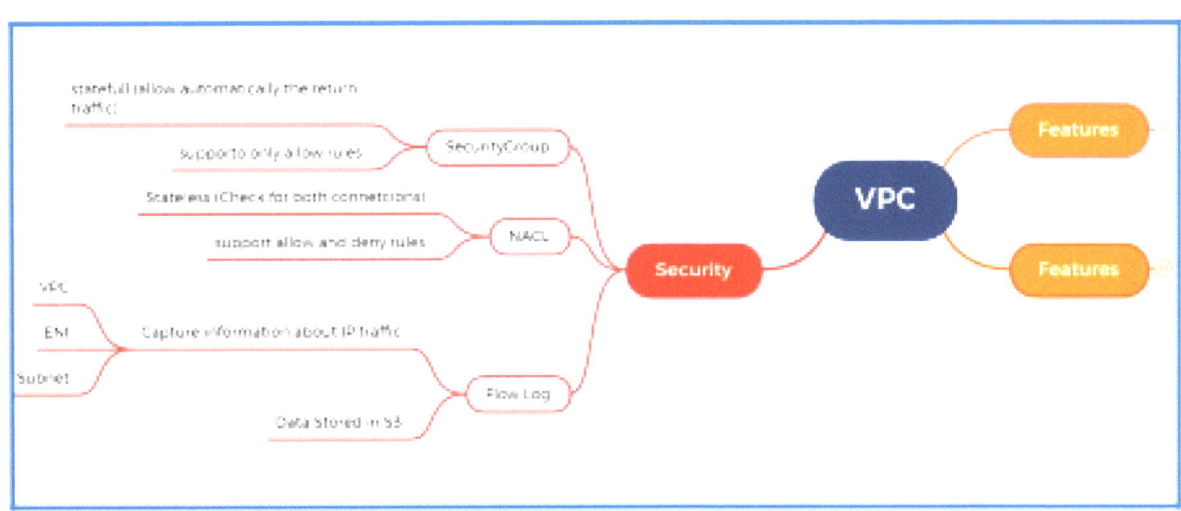

Features

VPC

Security

Features

- **NAT**
  - NAT instance
    - Connects instances with only Private IP to internet
    - Must be launched in a public subnet
    - Must have Elastic IP attached to it
    - Route tables must be configured
    - Unmanaged
    - Must be disable source destination check
  - NAT Gateway
    - Connects a Private network to internet
    - Live in a single AZ or Multiple AZ
    - Must be launched in a public subnet
    - Must have Elastic IP attached to it
    - Must be connected to Internet Gateway
    - Managed
- **VPC**
  - VPC Endpoints
    - Interface Endpoint
    - Gateway Endpoint
    - You connect to AWS services using a private network
  - VPC Peering
    - Connect two VPCs privately
    - Not overlapping CIDR
    - Is not transitive
    - Inter Region
    - Cross Account
- **VPN**
  - AWS site to site VPN
    - Encrypted connection over internet from on premises to VPC
    - AWS Virtual Hub
  - AWS Client VPN
    - Encrypted connection over internet to connect a PC to AWS VPC via VPN
- **AWS Direct Connect**
  - establishes a dedicated network connection or physical connection between your on premises network and AWS bypassing your internet service provider
  - Uses Direct Connect Gateway to connect multiple regions
- **AWS Transit Gateway**

VPC 2

- **VPC**
  - **Features**
  - **Security**
    - SecurityGroup
      - stateful (allow automatically the return traffic)
      - support to only allow rules
    - NACL
      - Stateless (Check for both connections)
      - support allow and deny rules
    - Flow Log
      - VPC
      - ENI
      - Subnet
      - Capture information about IP traffic
      - Data Stored in S3
  - **Features**

Availability

Region

Route 53

Amazon Route 53 is a highly available and scalable Domain Name System (DNS) web service

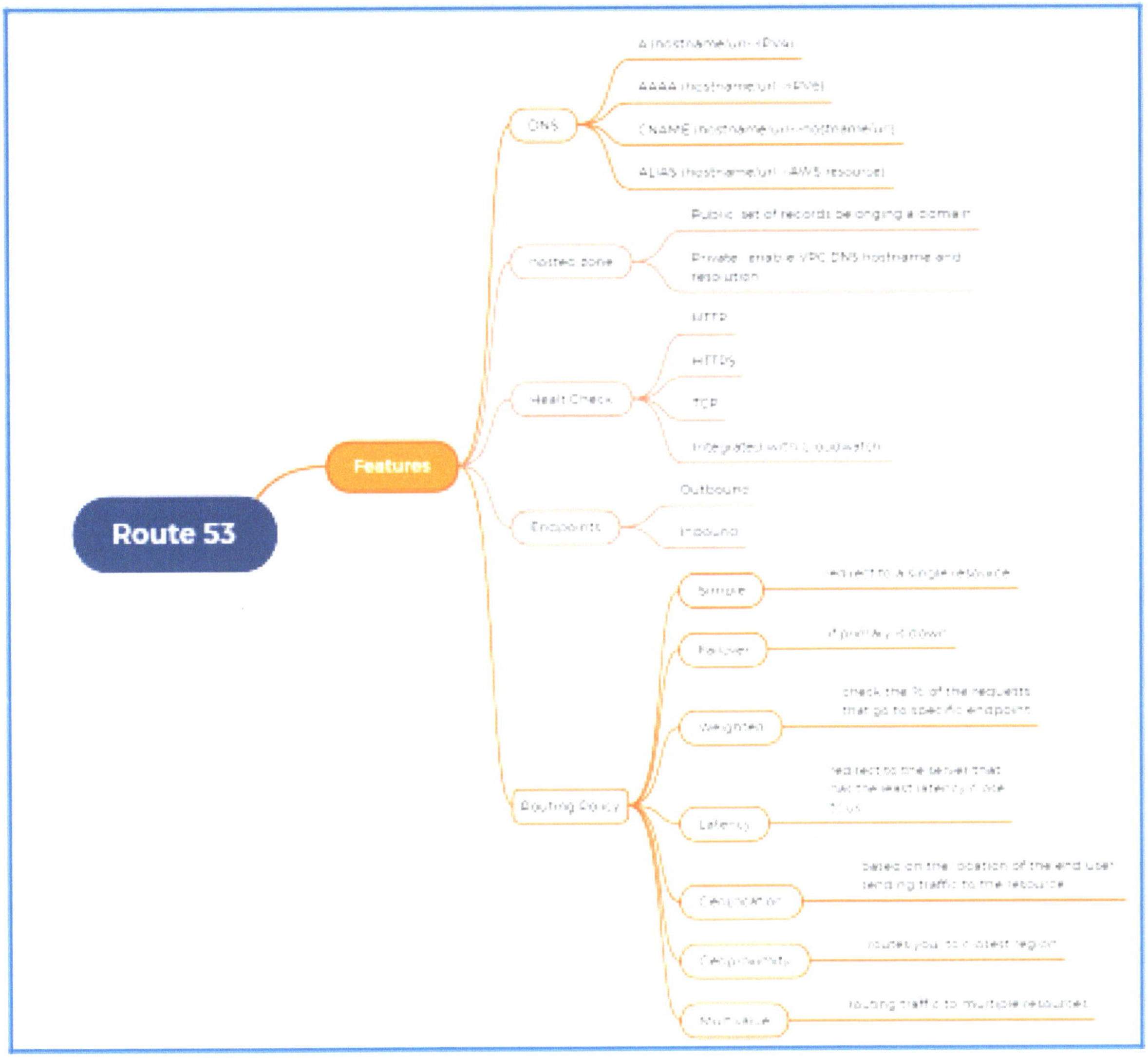

```
                                                          A (hostname/url - IPv4)
                                                          AAAA (hostname/url - IPv6)
                                              DNS         CNAME (hostname/url - hostname/url)
                                                          ALIAS (hostname/url - AWS resource)

                                                          Public: set of records belonging a domain
                                              hosted zone Private: enable VPC DNS hostname and
                                                          resolution

                                                          HTTP
                                                          HTTPS
                                              Healt Check tcp
                                                          Integrated with Cloudwatch

                                Features                  Outbound
                                              Endpoints   Inbound

    Route 53                                              Simple      route to a single resource

                                                          Failover    if primary is down

                                                          Weighted    check the % of the requests
                                                                      that go to specific endpoint

                                              Routing Policy           redirect to the server that
                                                          Latency      has the least latency in look
                                                                       it up

                                                          Geolocation  based on the location of the end user
                                                                       sending traffic to the resource

                                                          Geoproximity routes you to nearest region

                                                          Multivalue   routing traffic to multiple resources
```

Mind Map Route 53 1

Billing

50$ per month per hosted zone

Operations

Managed

CloudFront

Content Delivery Network.

Amazon CloudFront speeds up distribution of your static and dynamic web content, such as .html, .css, .php, image, and media files. When users request your content, CloudFront delivers it through a worldwide network of edge locations that provide low latency and high performance.

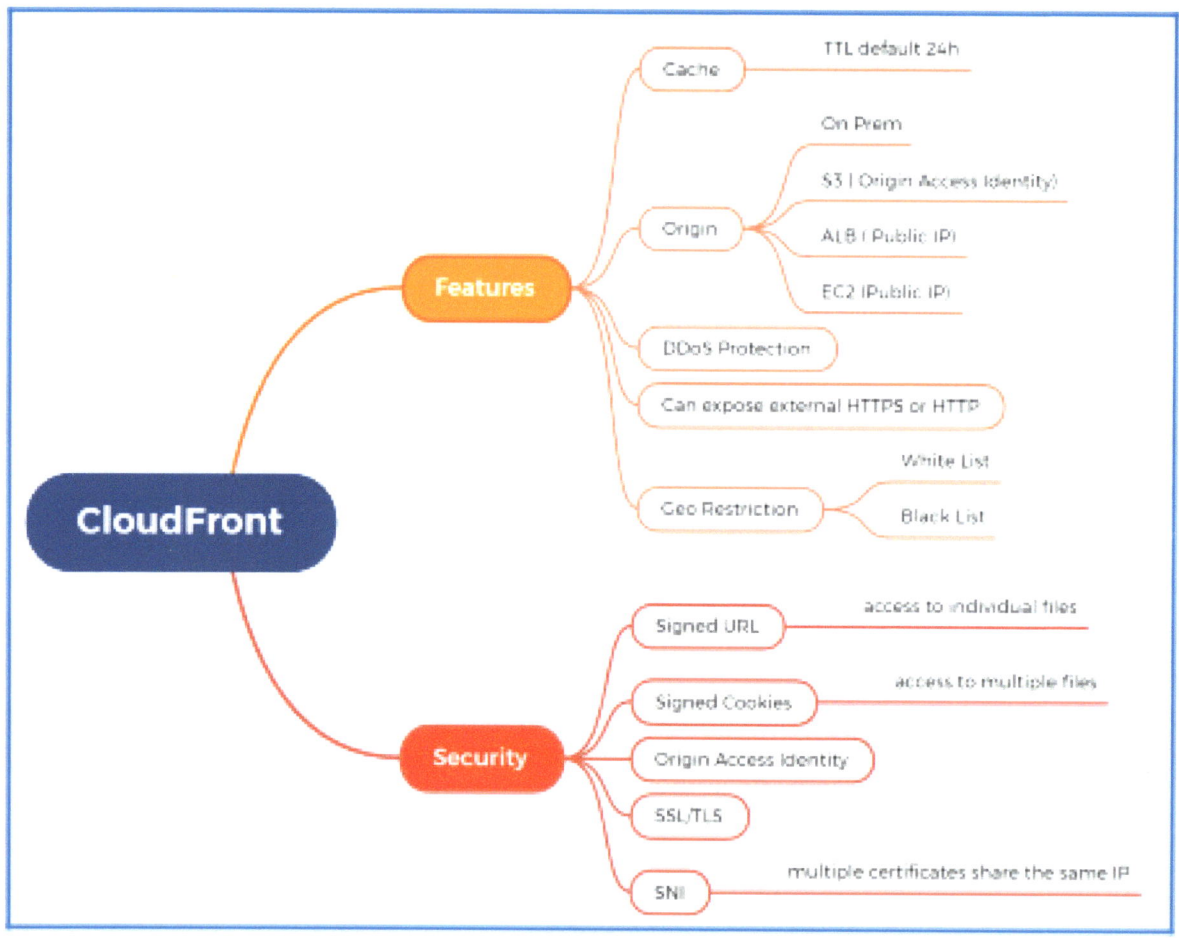

Mind Map CloudFront 1

Availability

Global (site in edge location)

AWS Global Accelerator

It routes the user traffic to the closet healthy application endpoint over the AWS global network.

AWS Global Accelerator route TCP and UDP traffic to healthy application endpoint in the closet AWS Region to the user. It intelligently route the traffic to the closet endpoint. It use anycast IP address (IP don't change when failover between region) so there are no issue with client cache.

Remember:

Unicast IP → 1 server=1 IP

Anycast IP→more servers have the same IP and the customer is directed to the closest one. Anycast IP send traffic to edge location and edge location send traffic to the application

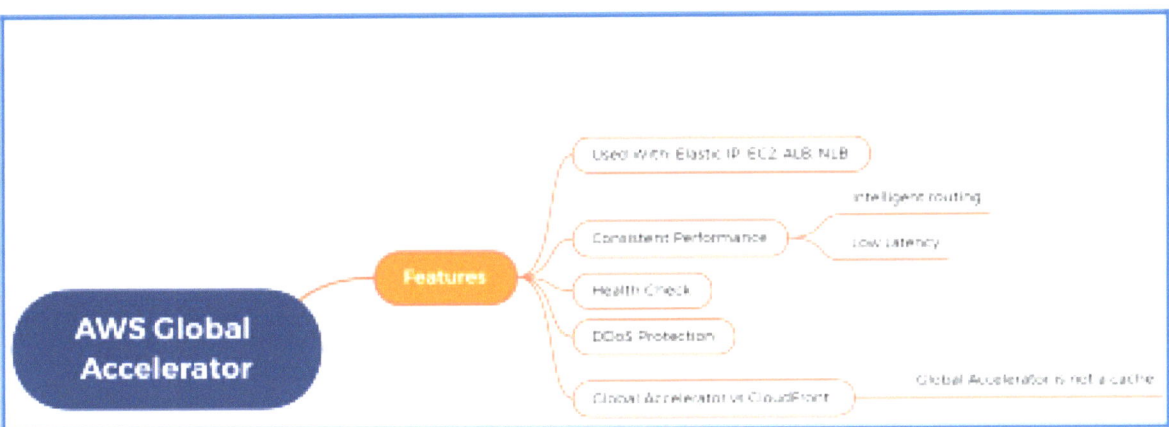

Mind Map Global Accelerator 1

ELB

Elastic Load Balancer automatically distributes your incoming traffic across multiple targets, such as EC2 instances, containers, and IP addresses, in one or more Availability Zones.

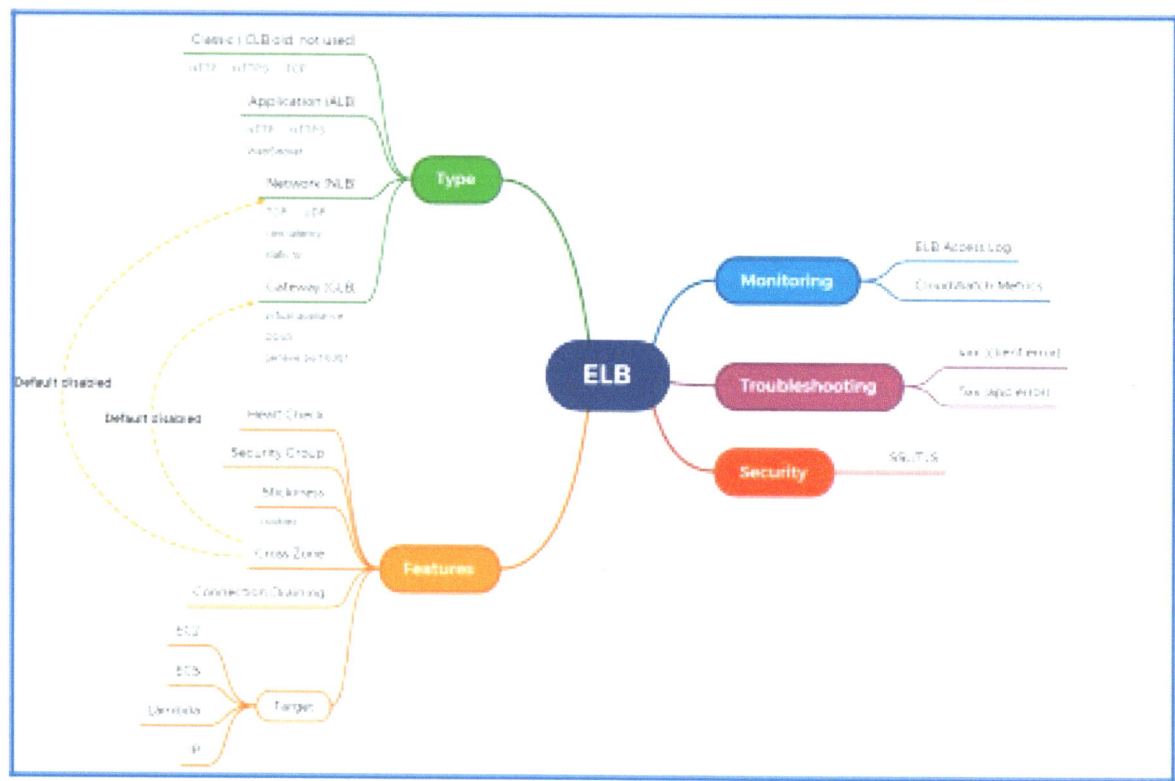

Mind Map ELB 1

Availability

AZ, multi AZ

Operations

Managed

ASG

Use Amazon EC2 Auto Scaling to automatically scale target services

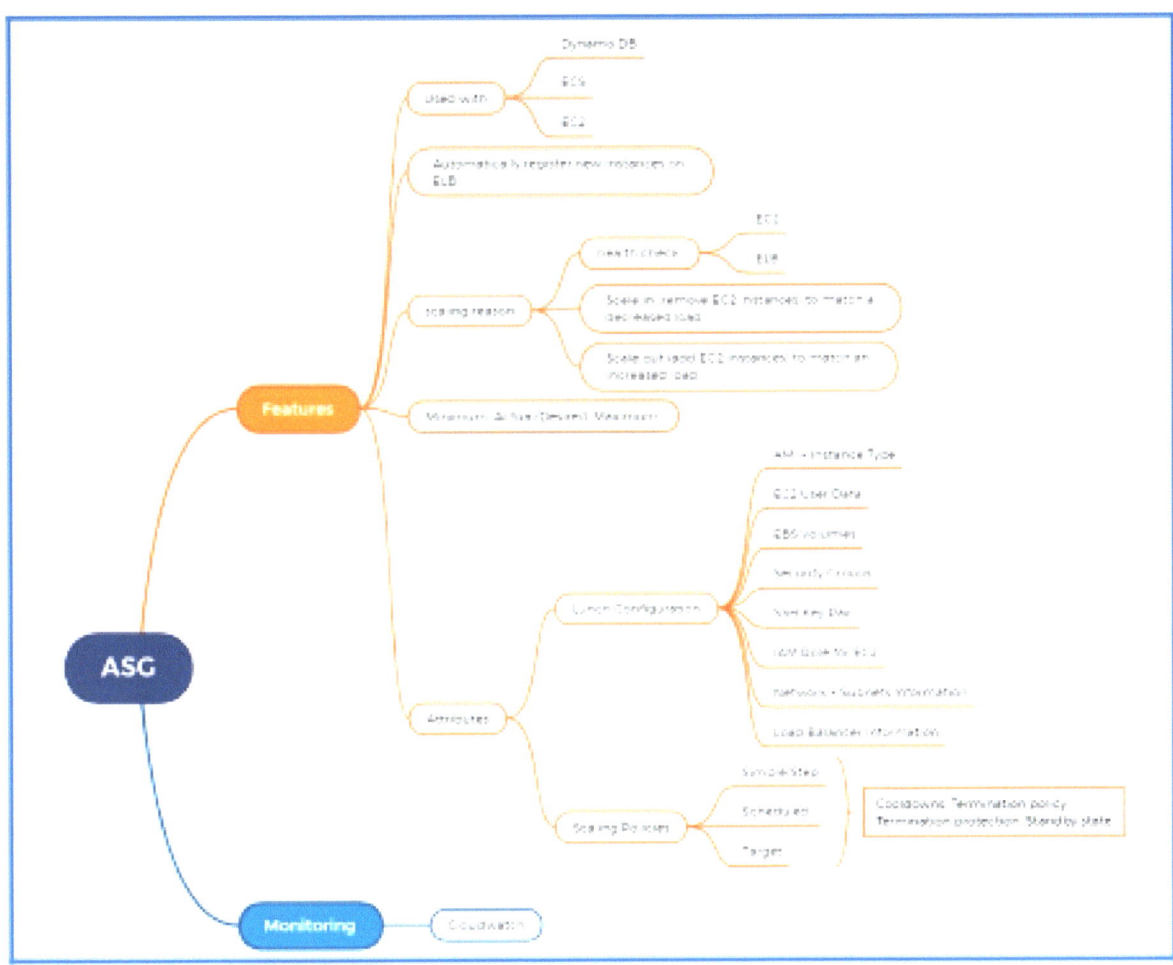

Mind Map ASG 1

Details:

To change the instance type:

1. instance stop
2. change instance type
3. instance restart

Billing

Free

Application

SQS

Messaging queue; store and forward patterns. Building distributed / decoupled applications

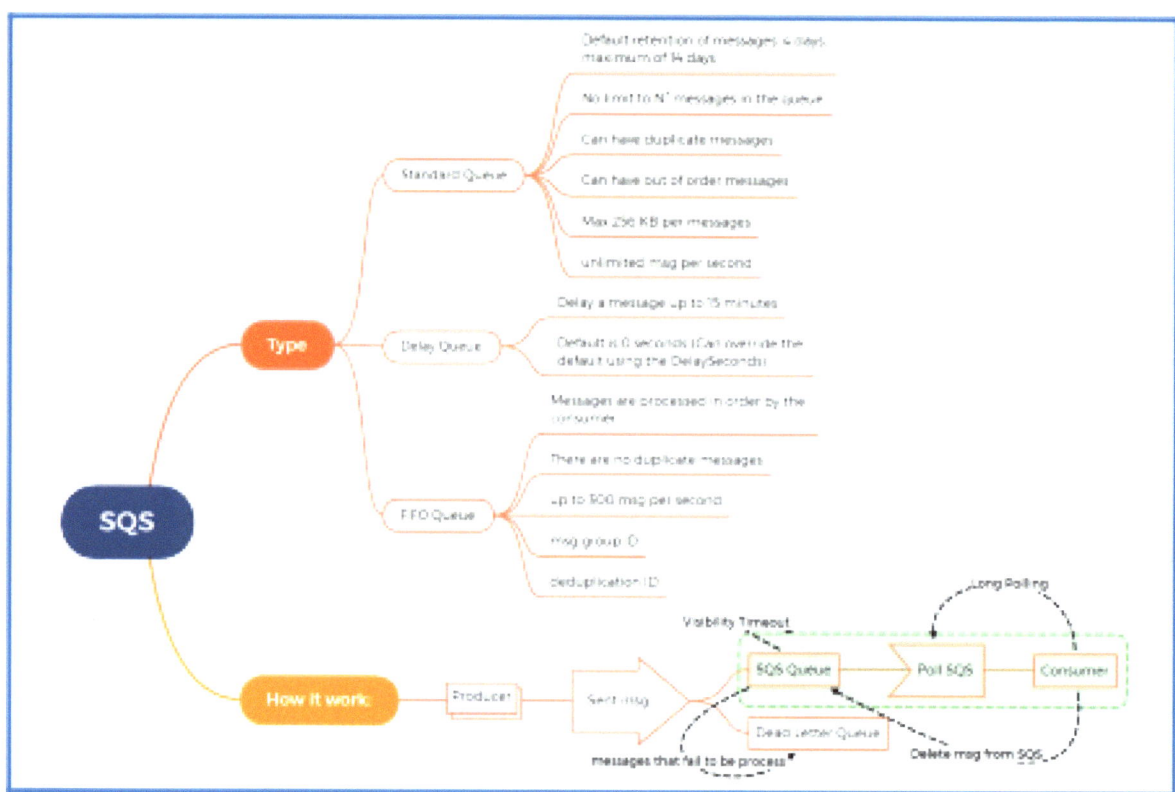

Mind Map SQS 1

Operations

Managed

Type

Pull, delete after consumed

SNS

Amazon Simple Notification Service (Amazon SNS) provides message delivery from publishers to subscribers (also known as producers and consumers).

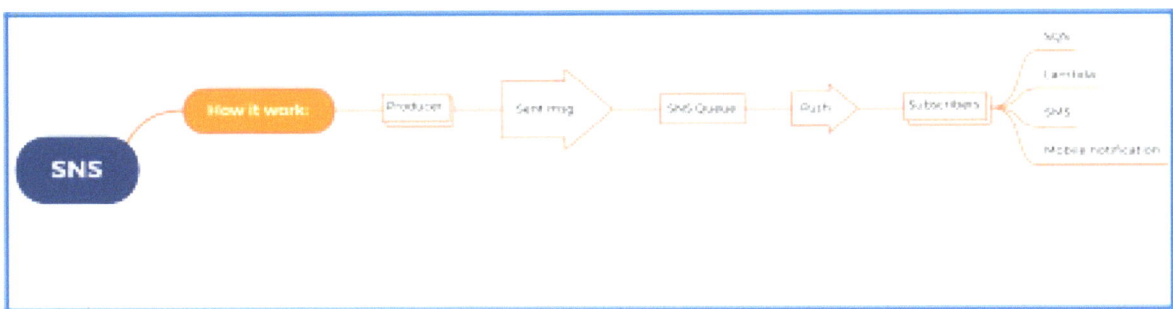

Mind Map SNS 1

Operations

Managed

Type

Push

Amazon MQ

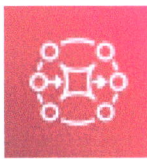

Migrate queue from on prem to cloud. Message broker service for Apache Active MQ and RabbitMQ

Step Functions

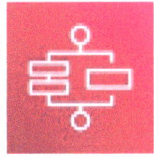

Out-of-the-box coordination of AWS service components with visual workflow. Order processing workflow

EventBridge

Amazon EventBridge is a serverless event bus that ingests data from your own apps, SaaS apps, and AWS services and routes that data to targets.

API Gateway

Amazon API Gateway enables you to create and deploy your own REST and WebSocket APIs at any scale

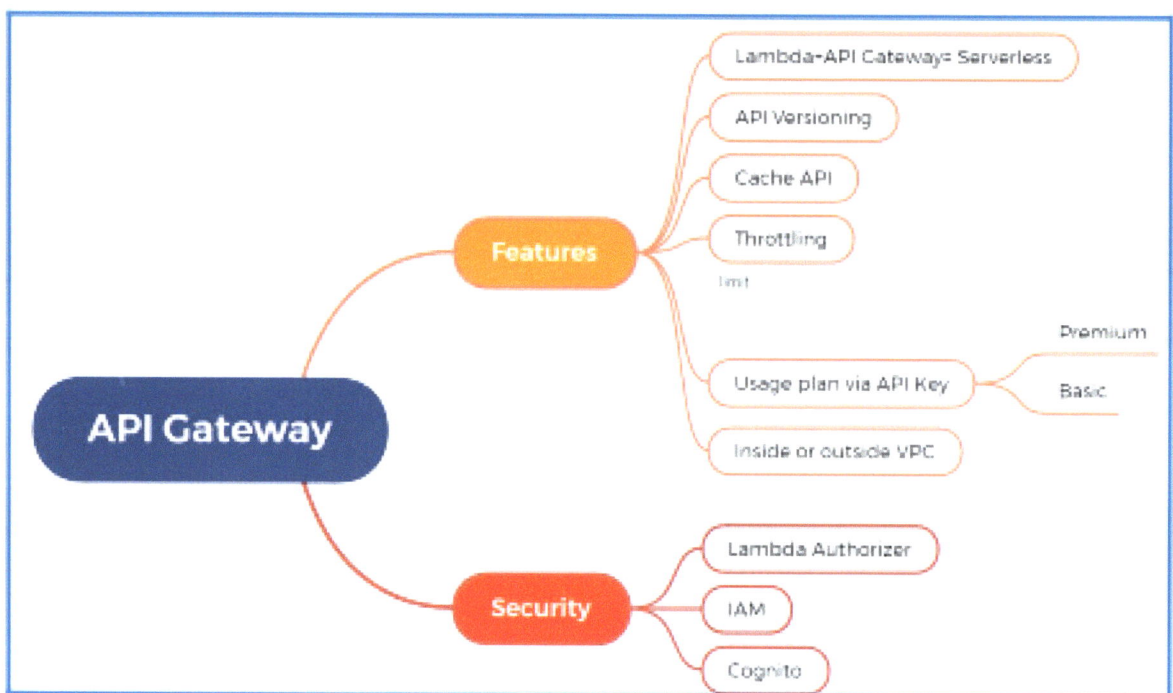

Mind Map API Gateway 1

Amplify

Tools and features for building full-stack application on AWS. Build web and mobile backend and web frontend

Appsync

AWS AppSync creates serverless GraphQL and Pub/Sub APIs that simplify application development through a single endpoint to securely query, update, or publish data

AWS Device Farm

AWS Device Farm is an application testing service that lets you improve the quality of your web and mobile apps by testing them across an extensive range of desktop browsers and real mobile devices; without having to provision and manage any testing infrastructure.

Rekognition

Provides automatic detection of objects appearing in pictures

Transcribe

Amazon Transcribe is an automatic speech recognition service that makes it easy to add speech to text capabilities to any application.

SageMaker

Amazon SageMaker is built on Amazon's two decades of experience developing real-world ML applications, including product recommendations, personalization, intelligent shopping, robotics, and voice-assisted devices. Build and deploy ML models.

Comprehend

Amazon Comprehend is a natural-language processing (NLP) service that uses machine learning to uncover valuable insights and connections in text. Natural Language Processing is a way for computers to analyze, understand, and derive meaning from textual information in a smart and useful way. Process the text to extract key phrase, entities for further analysis.

Lex

Amazon Lex is a fully managed artificial intelligence (AI) service for chatbot with advanced natural language models to design, build, test, and deploy conversational interfaces in applications.

TexTract

It is a fully ML service that automatically extracts test and data from scanned documents (pdf, image...)

Polly

Converting text to natural-sounding speech.

Elastic Transcoder

Transcodes video /file to various formats. New service name is MediaConverter

AppFlow

Automate bi-directional data flow between SAAS applications and AWS services.

Management & Governance

CloudFormation

AWS CloudFormation enables you to create and provision AWS infrastructure using a declarative method (template json or yaml). AWS CloudFormation enables you to use a template file to create and delete a collection of resources together as a single unit (a stack).

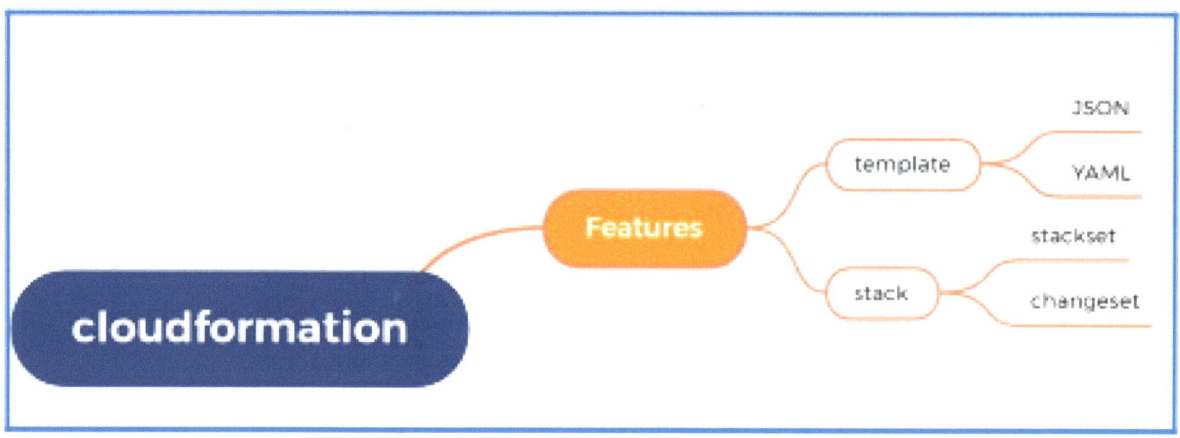

Mind Map CloudFormation 1

Billing:

Free

Beanstalk

With Elastic Beanstalk, you can quickly deploy and manage web applications (node js) running in EC2

Template format: WAR/ZIP

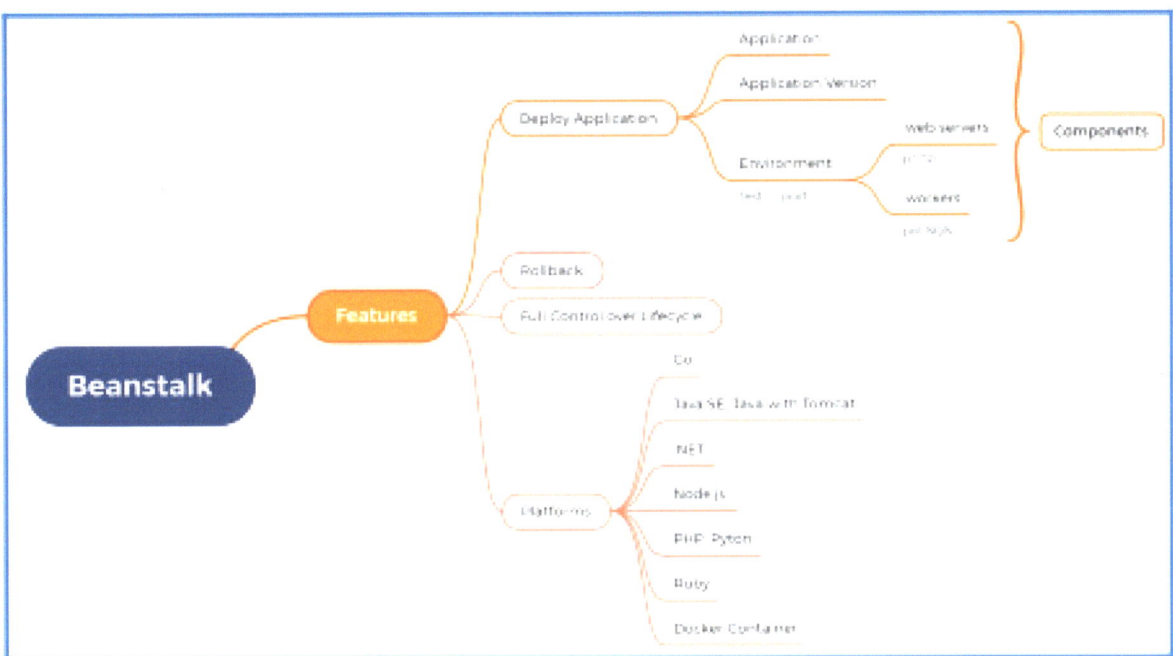

Mind Map Beanstalk 1

Operation:

Managed

Billing:

free but you pay for the underlying instances.

SSM Parameter Store

Parameter Store, a capability of AWS Systems Manager, provides secure, hierarchical storage for configuration data management and secrets management. Store data as password, license code, parameter value. Plaintext on encrypted. No key rotation

Config

AWS Config provides a detailed view of the resources associated with your AWS account, including how they are configured, how they are related to one another, and how the configurations and their relationships have changed over time.

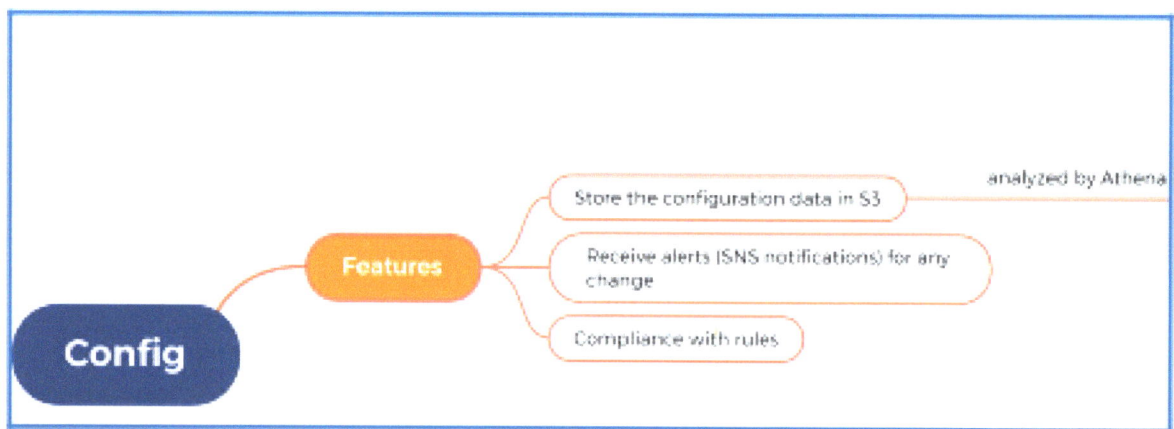

Mind Map Config 1

Availability:

Region

OpsWorks

AWS service that use Chef and Puppet to automate configuration management for EC2.

Resource Access Manager

AWS RAM helps you securely share your resources across AWS accounts, within your organization or organizational units (OUs). Use IAM roles and IAM users. The resources share are created with:

- AWS RAM Console
- RAM API
- AWS CLI
- AWS SDK for programmatically access

58

CloudWatch

Amazon CloudWatch provides a reliable, scalable, and flexible monitoring solution for every services in AWS.

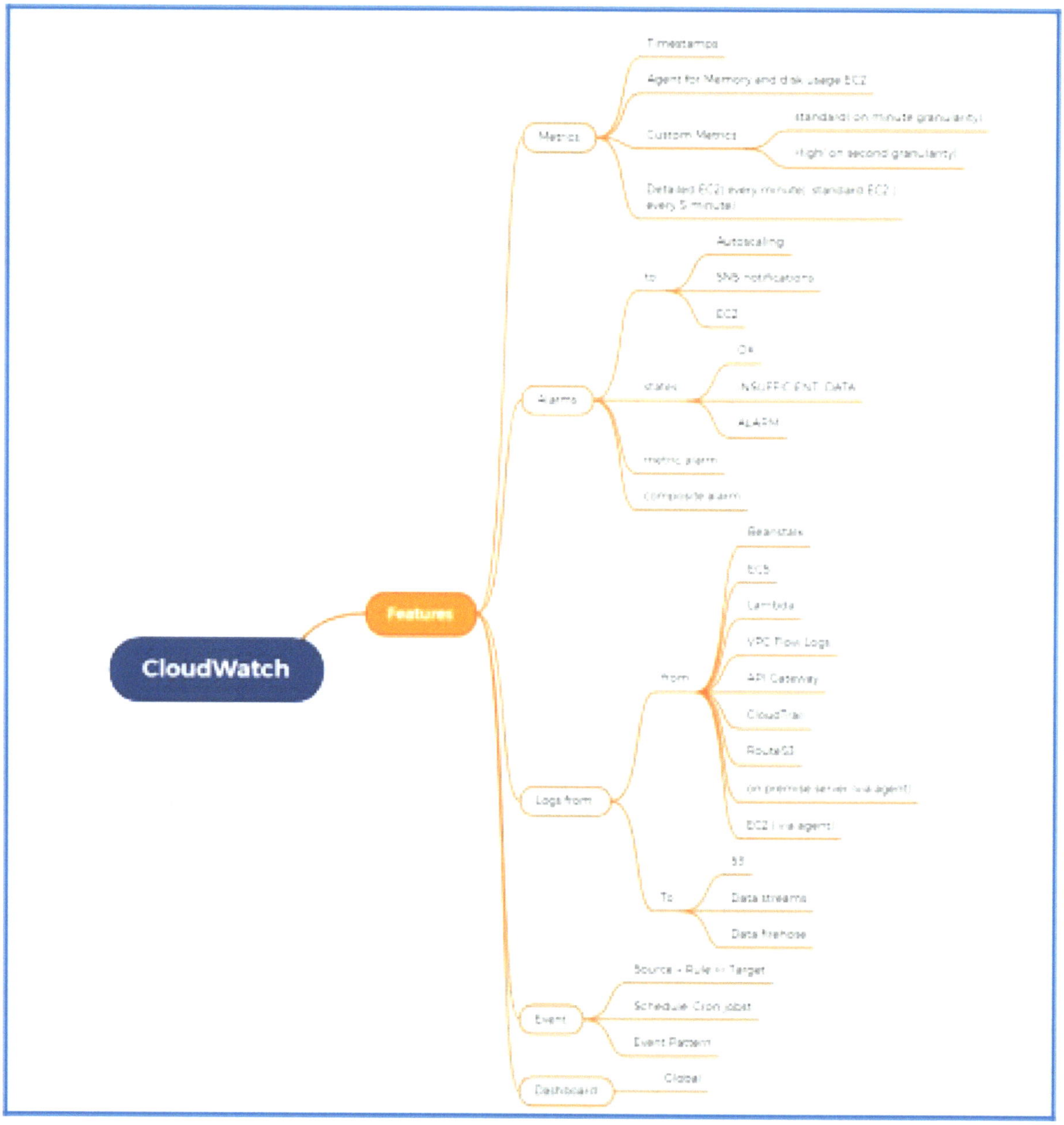

CloudWatch

Mind Map CloudWatch 1

CloudTrail

Provides governance, compliance and audit for your AWS Account. Log API activity. Log can be saved in S3
(for retained >90)

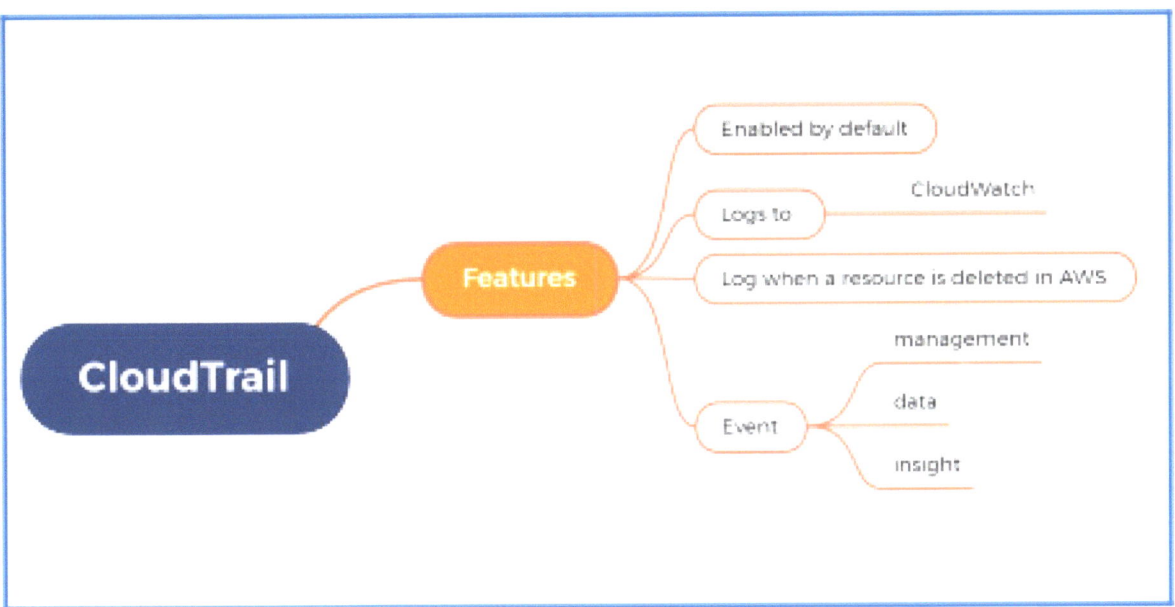

Mind Map CloudTrail 1

Event Bridge

EventBridge is a serverless service that uses events to connect application components together, making it easier for you to build scalable event-driven applications.

AWS X-Ray

AWS X-Ray provides a complete view of requests as they travel through your application and filters visual data across payloads, functions, traces, services, ...

Managed service for Prometeus

Amazon Managed Service for Prometheus is a Prometheus-compatible service that monitors and provides alerts on containerized applications and infrastructure

Managed Grafana

Amazon Managed Grafana is a fully managed service for Grafana, a popular open-source analytics platform that enables you to query, visualize data from DB

Security & Encryption

Encryption in flight (HTTPS/SSL)

Serve side encryption at rest

Client side encryption

Secrets Manager

AWS Secrets Manager helps you to securely encrypt, store, and retrieve credentials for your databases and other services.

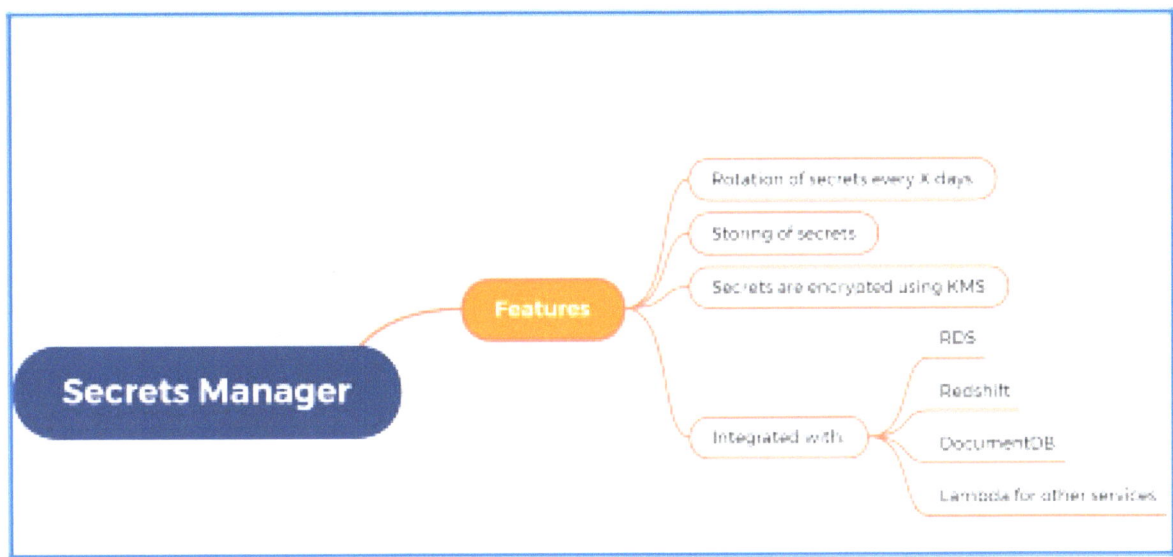

Secrets Manager 1

Billing:

per secret

AWS Directory Service

AWS Directory Service for Microsoft Active Directory lets you connect your AWS resources with an existing on-premises directory, or set up a new standalone

Simple AD <5000 users

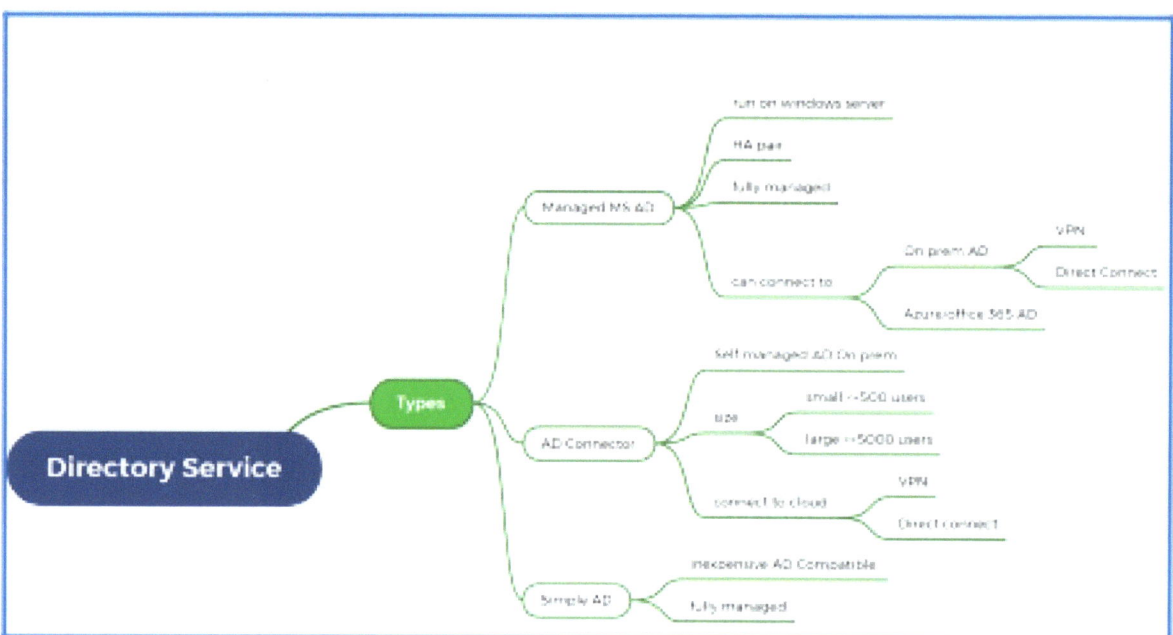

Mind Map Directory Service 1

Identity Federation

Allows users outside of AWS to take on a temporary role to access AWS resources. Using federation, you don't need to create IAM users.

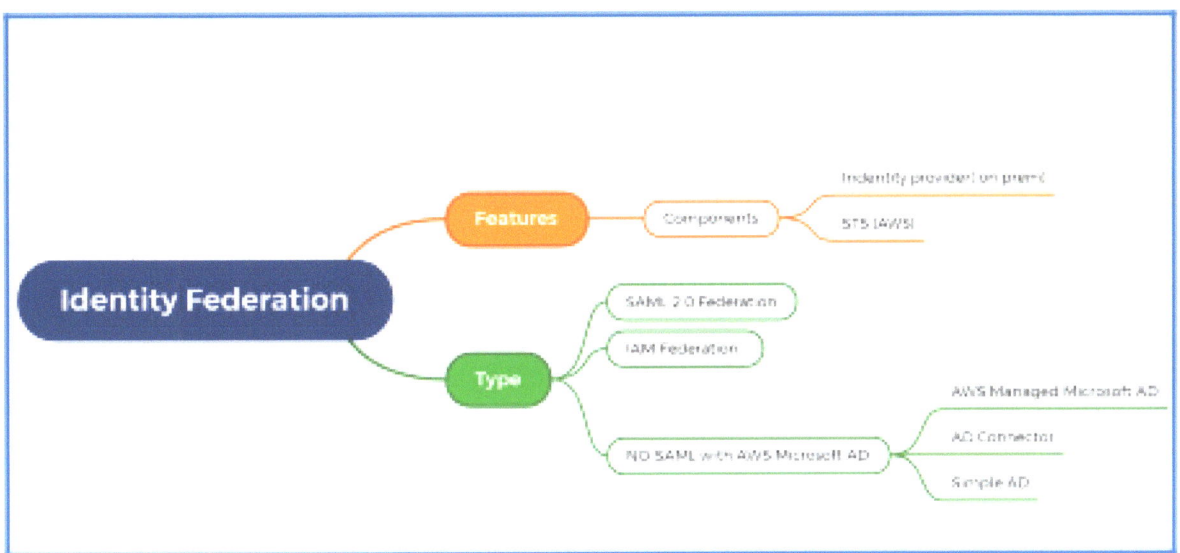

Mind Map Identity Federation 1

SSO

IAM Identity Center helps you securely create, or connect, your workforce identities and manage their access centrally across AWS accounts and applications

Cognito

Amazon Cognito handles user authentication and authorization for your web and mobile apps.

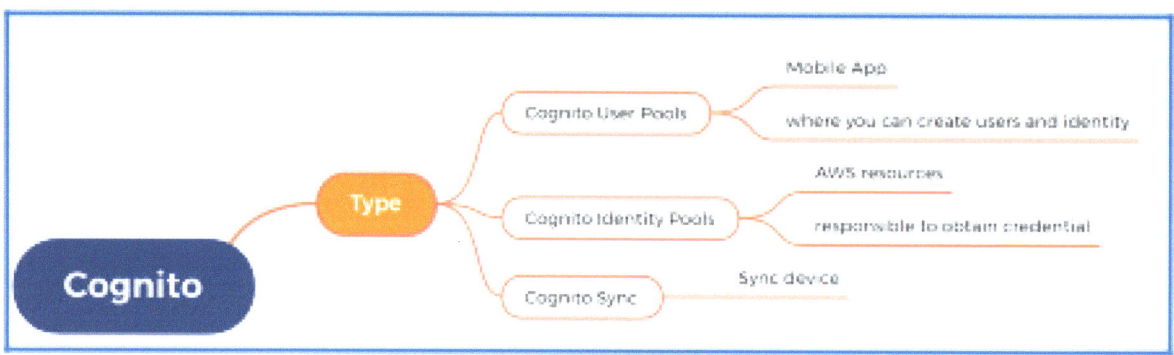

Mind Map Cognito 1

KMS

AWS Key Management Service (AWS KMS) is an encryption and key management service.

AWS Key Management Service (AWS KMS) lets you create, manage, and control cryptographic keys across your applications and AWS services.

multitenant

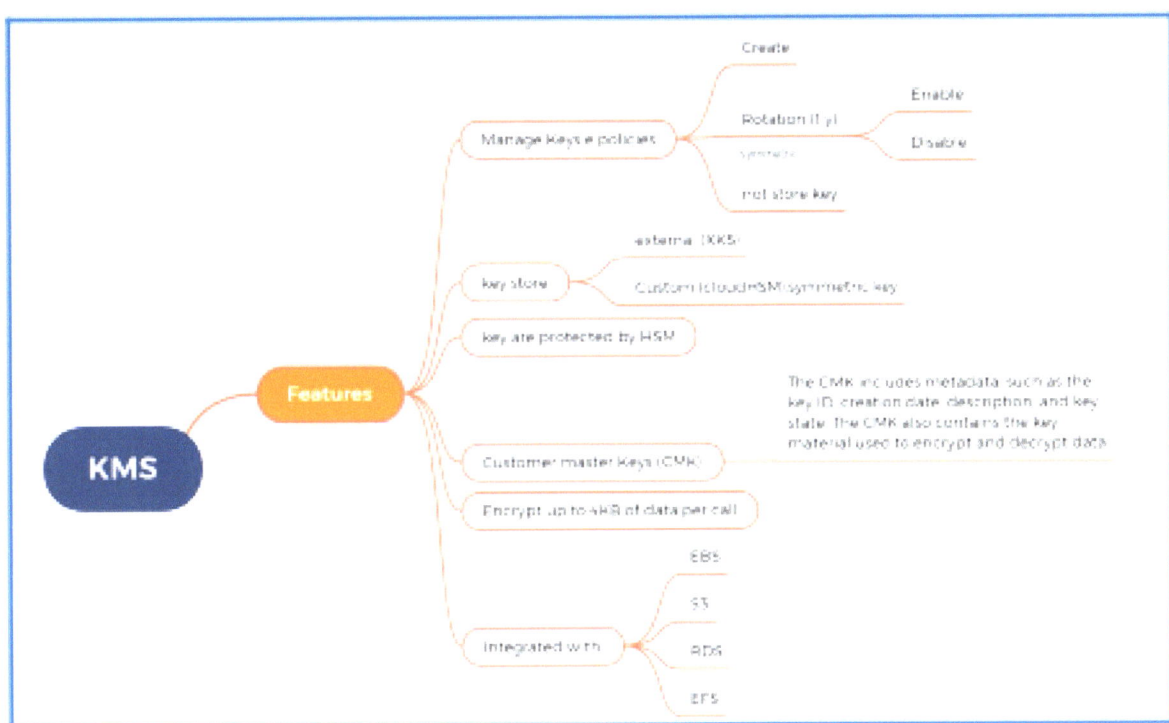

Mind Map KMS 1

CloudHSM

AWS CloudHSM offers secure cryptographic key storage for customers by providing managed hardware security modules.

Single tenant

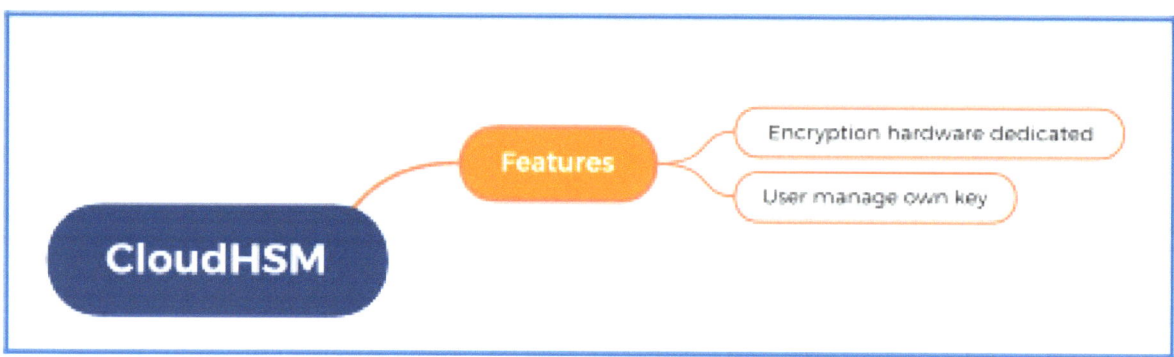

CloudHSM 1

Certificate Manager

Use AWS Certificate Manager (ACM) to provision, manage, and deploy public and private SSL/TLS certificates for use with AWS services and your internal connected resources.

Create store and renew certificate.

WAF

AWS WAF is a web application firewall that lets you monitor web requests, traffic flow inspection and to create rules to filter web traffic

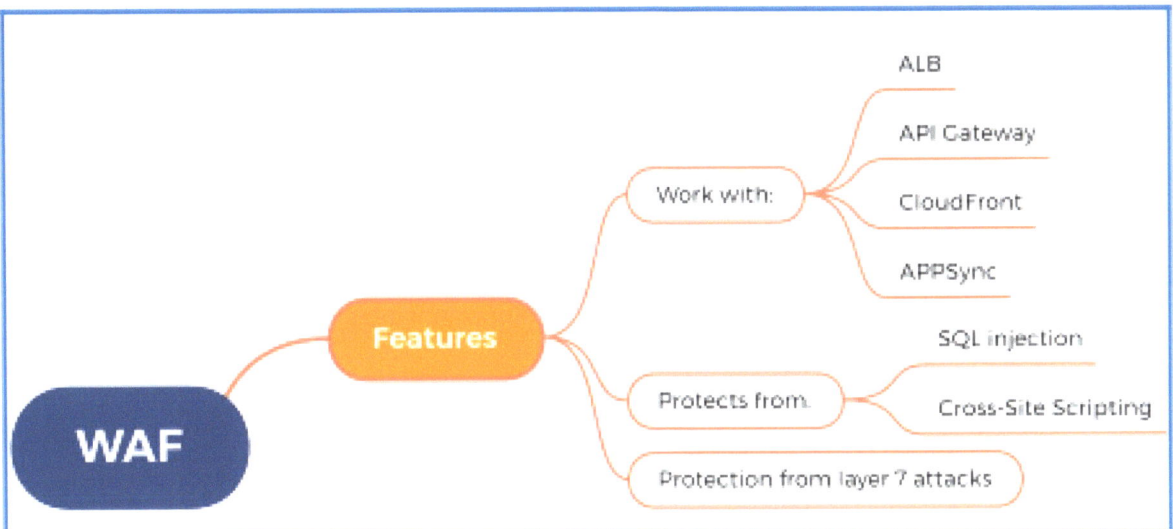

WAF 1

Shield

AWS provides protection on DDoS attacks

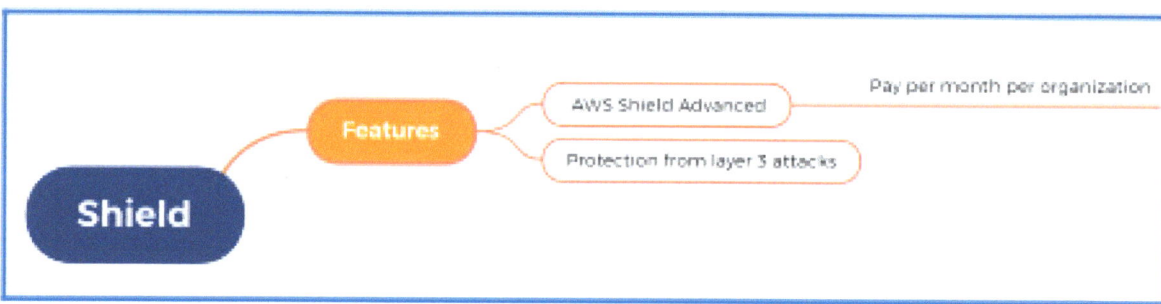

Shield 1

- **Billing**: free

Inspector

Allows you to perform automated security assessments on your applications.

Macie

Amazon Macie is a data security service that uses machine learning (ML) and pattern matching to discover and help protect your sensitive data.

GuardDuty

Amazon GuardDuty is a continuous security monitoring service. Amazon GuardDuty can help to identify unexpected and potentially unauthorized or malicious activity in your AWS environment. It provides intelligent threat detection for AWS products and services. It monitors all traffic. It can not Take action directly.

Pricing and Support

Pricing Calculator

AWS Pricing Calculator lets you explore AWS services and create an estimate for the cost of your use cases on AWS.

Budgets

Is a tool that you can use to set thresholds for your AWS service usage and costs.

Cost allocation tags

A tag is a label that you or AWS assigns to an AWS resource. Each tag consists of a key and a value. For each resource, each tag key must be unique, and each tag key can have only one value. You can use tags to organize your resources, and cost allocation tags to track your AWS costs on a detailed level

Cost Explorer

Is a tool that you can use to visualize, understand, and manage your AWS costs and usage over time.

Cost & Usage Report

The AWS Cost and Usage Reports (AWS CUR) contains the most comprehensive set of cost and usage data available. You can use Cost and Usage Reports to publish your AWS billing reports to an Amazon Simple Storage Service (Amazon S3) bucket that you own. You can receive reports that break down your costs by the hour, day, or month, by product or product resource, or by tags that you define yourself. AWS updates the report in your bucket once a day in comma-separated value (CSV) format.

Price List API

Query the price of AWS services

Support Plans
Aws Support.

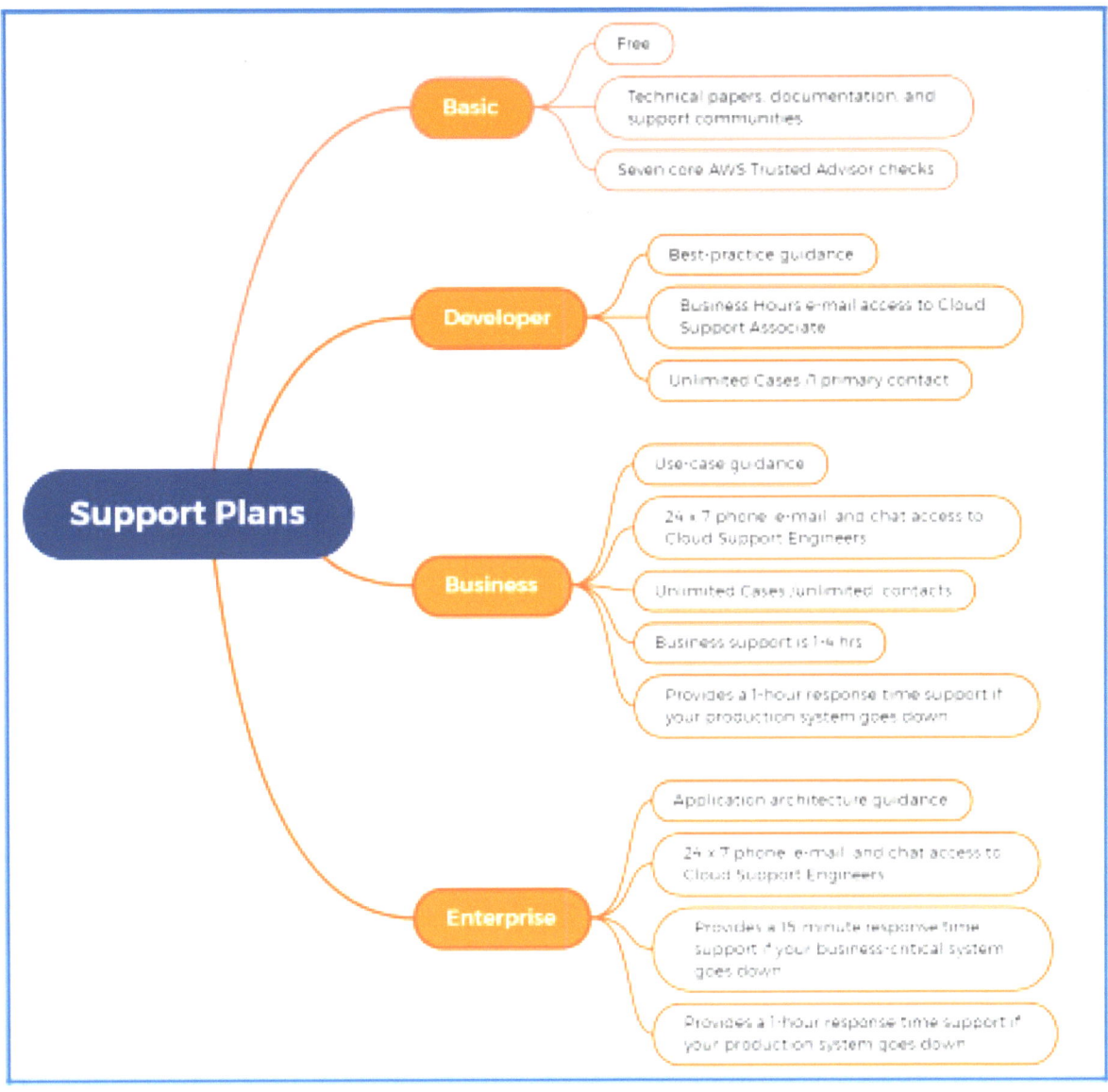

Mind Map Support Plans 1

License Manager

License Manager makes it easier for you to manage your software licenses from vendors, such as Microsoft, SAP, Oracle, and IBM, across AWS and your on-premises environments.

Compute optimizer

AWS Compute Optimizer helps avoid overprovisioning and underprovisioning four types of AWS resources —Amazon Elastic Compute Cloud (EC2) instance types, Amazon Elastic Block Store (EBS) volumes, Amazon Elastic Container Service (ECS) services on AWS Fargate, and AWS Lambda functions—based on your utilization data.

Marketplace

AWS Marketplace is a digital catalog that provides listings of third-party software that runs on AWS.

Quick Start

Quick Starts are built by AWS solutions architects and partners to help you deploy popular technologies on AWS, based on AWS best practices for security and high availability. These accelerators reduce hundreds of manual procedures into just a few steps, so you can build your production environment quickly and start using it immediately.

OpsWorks

AWS service that use Chef and Puppet to automate configuration management for EC2.

AWS Partner Network (APN)

The AWS Partner Network (APN) is focused on helping partners build successful AWS-based businesses to drive superb customer experiences.

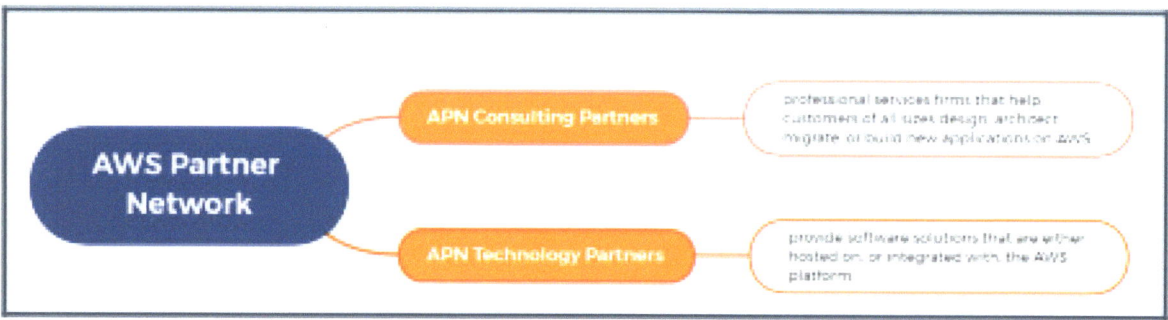

Mind Map AWS Partner Network (APN) 1

Professional Services

AWS Professional Services shares a collection of offerings to help you achieve specific outcomes related to enterprise cloud adoption.

Migration and Innovation

Cloud Adoption Framework

Provides advice to your company to enable a quick and smooth migration to AWS.

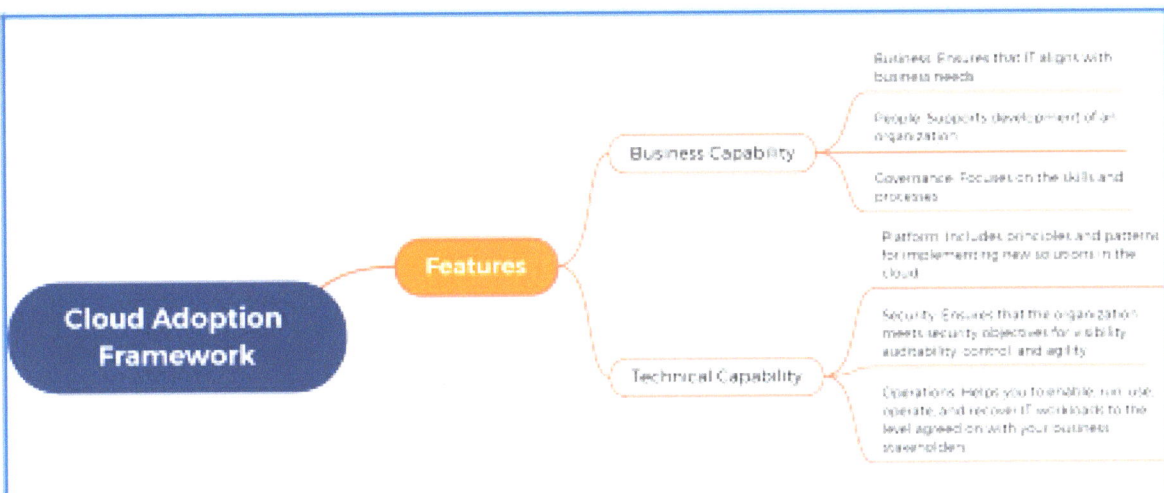

Mind Map AWS Cloud Adoption Framework 1

Migration strategies

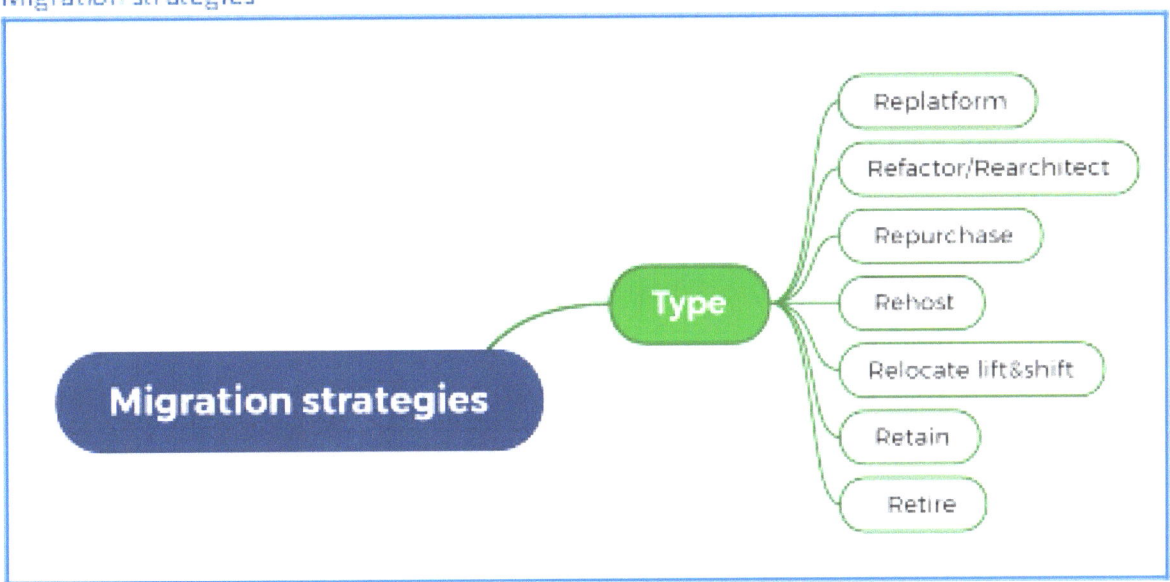

Mind Map AWS Migration strategies 1

Well-Architected Framework

The Well-Architected Framework helps you understand how to design and operate reliable, secure, efficient, and cost-effective systems in the AWS Cloud.

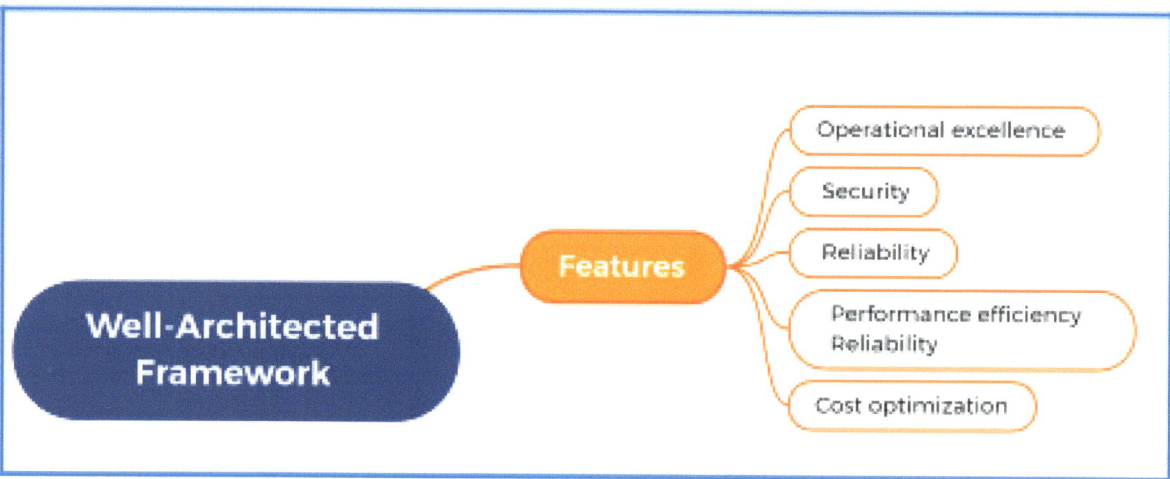

Mind Map Well-Architected Framework 1

Application Discovery Service

AWS Application Discovery Service helps you plan cloud migration projects by gathering information about your on-premises data centers.

Agentless→ Vmware

Agent based→ other

Server migration service

Product Update: We recommend AWS Application Migration Service (AWS MGN) as the primary migration service for lift-and-shift migrations. AWS Application Migration Service (AWS MGN) is the primary migration service recommended for lift-and-shift migrations to AWS. Customers currently using Server Migration Service (SMS) are encouraged to switch to Application Migration Service for future migrations

AWS DataSync

AWS DataSync moves large amounts of data online between on-premises storage and Amazon S3, Amazon Elastic File System (Amazon Elastic File System) or Amazon FSx.

Agent connected to storage on prem

Database Migration Service

Migrate relational databases, nonrelational databases, and other types of data stores to AWS.

AWS Database Migration Service (AWS DMS) is a managed migration and replication service that helps move your database and analytics workloads to AWS quickly, securely, and with minimal downtime and zero data loss.

Reference

https://docs.aws.amazon.com/

Exam test

Free & Accurate Amazon AWS Certified Solutions Architect - Associate SAA-C03 Practice Questions | Exam Topics

www.ingramcontent.com/pod-product-compliance
Lightning Source LLC
LaVergne TN
LVHW071523070326
832902LV00003B/66